SIMPLE_COMPLEXITY

SIMPLE_
COMPLEXĪTY

A Management Book for the Rest of Us:
A Guide to Systems Thinking

WILLIAM DONALDSON, PhD

NEW YORK

NASHVILLE • MELBOURNE • VANCOUVER

SIMPLE_COMPLEXITY
A Management Book for the Rest of Us:
A Guide to Systems Thinking

Published in New York, New York, by Morgan James Publishing. Morgan James is a trademark of Morgan James, LLC. www.MorganJamesPublishing.com

The Morgan James Speakers Group can bring authors to your live event. For more information or to book an event visit The Morgan James Speakers Group at www.TheMorganJamesSpeakersGroup.com.

ISBN 978-1-68350-074-2 paperback
ISBN 978-1-68350-075-9 eBook
ISBN 978-1-68350-076-6 hardcover
Library of Congress Control Number: 2016907525

Cover Design by:
Megan James

Interior Design by:
Bonnie Bushman
The Whole Caboodle Graphic Design

In an effort to support local communities, raise awareness and funds, Morgan James Publishing donates a percentage of all book sales for the life of each book to Habitat for Humanity Peninsula and Greater Williamsburg.

Get involved today! Visit
www.MorganJamesBuilds.com

Table of Contents

Preface

All organizations are perfectly designed to get the results they are now getting.
—Tom Northup[1]

Think about that statement. It is indisputable. Your enterprise is a system that converts inputs—time, people, and money—into outputs—goods and services. The system must be perfectly designed to get the results it is getting today, for it cannot be otherwise. However, are those results acceptable and desired? Did you design the system, or did it just develop by default? As the owner or leader, you are the designer of your organization. You are the architect, the engineer, the artist, the philosopher king who designs the system—or not! There is what I call an Enterprise Management System (EMS) already in place in your company. As you will see, it has to be there. However, is it *your* management system? Did you design it? Did it just develop over time, or did you inherit it from a prior management regime, prior owner, or family member?

I was meeting with the owner of a successful services company and we were talking about her business. She had read many of the popular management books and had implemented much of the advice. She had rigorously evaluated her sales, marketing, accounting, and other management disciplines. She was sensitive to her corporate culture and her people and felt her company was on sound footing. She was arguably a great success story. She had done all of the things managers and owners are advised to do.

The owner did all this, and yet, she told me "something is missing." She felt "the business ran her." She said, "The sum of the parts is less than the whole." She wondered how, having worked so hard on all of the parts of her company, the company could still feel so disjointed. I asked her two simple questions. "What about the system that encompasses all of those discrete systems you told me about? Did that develop by default, or did you design it?"

She was taken aback. It had never occurred to her there was a larger system at work, controlling all of the discrete systems she had worked so hard to perfect. As we talked further, she realized she had let *that* system develop by default. The system that housed all the discrete elements had developed by default as she constructed all the subordinate systems. Even though she was at the center of that *greater* system, the fact was, she knew little about it.

So, what are we to do about the system that encompasses all of those discrete systems? What are we to do about our *enterprise* system? Yes, it too is a system. As you will come to see, every organization is a system—in fact, a system of systems, perfectly designed to get the results it is getting today. You must become intimately familiar with *your* enterprise system. You must come to feel its rhythms, predict its behaviors, and plan its evolution.

We will explore these questions and concepts in *Simple_Complexity*. We will explore how systems are both simple and complex and why you have to embrace both states. The system already at work in your enterprise is highly complex, and you must learn to deal with that complexity. However, in order to do so, you must simplify your thinking about the enterprise, while not losing sight of the complexity. Margaret Wheatley in her illuminating book *Leadership and the New Science* puts it thusly: "The layers of complexity, the sense of things being beyond our control and out of control, are but signals of our failure to understand a deeper reality of organizational life."[2]

If you have studied business, you know that it is taught in a reductionist way, breaking a complex business into smaller pieces—marketing, management, operations, finance, accounting, leadership, and so on. Modeled on Newtonian and mechanical principles, this method of teaching presumes that if we study all the parts individually, we will understand the whole. Academics and consultants encourage us to systematize our processes and methods for repeatability and predictability. Just like the owner I describe above, we have dutifully complied. We rationalize and optimize our companies for point-of-sale, product development, leadership development, and so on. We have read about leadership, organizational behavior, and planning, and tried to optimize these areas of our business. We have attended seminars on finance, operations, supply chain, marketing, and a host of other management topics and returned to our companies to implement our learning. These efforts are all important, but they stem from a reductionist view of the business that assumes we can reduce the business to its component parts and optimize those, and thereby optimize the whole. However, systems *do not* work that way. Systems take on a life, a rhythm, and behaviors of their own. Without the benefit of systems thinking, systems can appear to be daunting and overwhelming.

Systems thinking has been recommended and promulgated by some of the leading management thinkers of our time—Peter Senge, Peter Drucker, Margaret Wheatley, Donella Meadows, W. Edwards Deming, and others. I commend to you their works and the works of the originators, among them Plato, Whitehead, von Bertalanffy, Ackoff, Churchman, Checkland, Forrester, and others. Yet, most managers have not trained in systems thinking. They merely try to manage the system as best they can without this important knowledge. I wrote *Simple_Complexity* to give you that knowledge. I believe systems thinking is the unifying discipline that brings clarity to all of the other disciplines at work in your enterprise.

More specifically, this book will help you purposefully design an Enterprise Management System that fits your enterprise, your enterprise's style, the current moment in the market cycle, the reality the enterprise resides in, the reality within which it interacts, and your own style. If you are a manager and cannot design your own Enterprise Management System, my hope is that *Simple_Complexity* will give you a new set of lenses through which to view your existing enterprise system and to achieve a deeper understanding of the system in which you work and manage, thereby making you more effective.

In other words, this is a management book for the rest of us, for every owner or entrepreneur, son or daughter, department manager or division general manager thrown into the deep end of heading an enterprise or part thereof. Most management books are written by celebrity CEOs who have run major corporations, by academics who theorize about how to run a major corporation or function therein, or by consultants who use anecdotes and inference to project wisdom or insight. Many are well written and often compelling, *if* you already have the context and viewpoint of the CEO managing a major corporation or if you have spent countless hours contemplating how you would do that. Most of us do not have this luxury. I have been tremendously fortunate in my career to have done all three for long periods. I have been the CEO of many companies, including an international joint venture and a publicly traded company. I have consulted with dozens of boards and CEOs, and I have taught management for decades.

Additionally, many management books are predicated on the fact that you just have not been exposed to the *one* true way to manage your company or entity, and if you will only heed the advice of the author, you will emerge triumphant. If you will only employ the technique the author is selling, your worries will be over. I have seen enough companies and had enough successes and failures to know that there is no one-size-fits-all solution.

Finally, many management books look at only one small, albeit important, part of the enterprise. They explore leadership, or culture, or sales, or supply chain and seek to optimize those systems. These are important and worthy endeavors. However, they are all subordinate to the *enterprise* system. They are each a system within a larger system. As you will see later in the book, optimizing these discrete systems is often counterproductive.

Based on my struggles to run my own companies, my attempt to view and model the enterprise as a system, and my academic research into the management of systems, I have come to believe there is a simple set of principles behind how humankind has dealt with systems and businesses—an archetype. You do not need to reinvent a new system of management. I believe an archetypal management system is already at work in your enterprise. You merely have to see it and embrace it. I believe that if you will look with the benefit of some new lenses, systems-thinking lenses, you will see clearly the system elements and dynamics shaping your enterprise.

I hope to give you the tools you need to understand, engineer, and lead your business without the benefit of an advanced degree or years of corporate experience. The concepts we will discuss are not complex; in fact, they are by design simple. However, they are profound and powerful. Also, even though the concepts are not complex, they are not necessarily easy to implement. My sincere hope is that when you have finished reading this book, you will say, "Now *that* makes sense. Now that I see and understand the system dynamics swirling around me, I can do this." You will have the confidence and clarity to design your own management system, and not have to rely on one from some stranger in a different business. Years ago, I taught a public session where I presented the basics of this book. At the start of this session, I had the attendees introduce themselves. During the introductions, I asked the individuals to tell the other attendees what kept them up at night as leaders, managers, CEOs, and owners. A young woman who was executive director of a not-for- profit said she was feeling overwhelmed by her role as CEO and was struggling for clarity in her work and her overall work-life balance. She stated that she was considering resigning due to her feelings of uncertainty and stress. At the end of the session, I asked attendees to share their learning and "aha" moments. Hers was a particularly revealing and rewarding postscript. She said, "I am going to go and get my life back. I now see the extent of the system, I understand that I am the engineer and architect of that system, and I am going to go and design the system we need, one that I understand and can control. I know the problems inside and outside of my organization will not get any easier, but I now feel that I can design a system of management that can help me better cope with the challenges." I hope the principles you will learn in this book can help you gain that clarity, that sense of being in control, and that level of courage and resolve as well.

How to Use This Book

A great deal has been written about the individual management topics I cover in *Simple_Complexity*. Much of it is brilliant, and I have used and cited it herein. However, I have tried not to rehash this prior work. I commend you to the readings of others on these topics. For convenience, I have provided a recommended reading list at the end of each chapter. I encourage you to explore these excellent resources for the wisdom and clarity they will bring in light of a systems-thinking approach. Rather than recite the wisdom already provided, I have tried to expand upon this wisdom and bring it all into focus using a new set of lenses, lenses provided by systems thinking. Once you have seen and embraced the enterprise system, this prior work in the subordinate systems will be invaluable.

Simple_Complexity is broken into three parts. Part 1 will introduce you to the power of systems and systems thinking. In Chapter 1, we will explore the intriguing, circular nature of systems, complexity, and holistic thought. In Chapter 2, we will explore the concept of the enterprise as a system. In Chapter 3, we will explore how your current system came into being, look at the foundations of that system, and contemplate a vexing management paradox that you must understand.

Part 2 explores the Enterprise Management System more deeply. First, in Chapter 4, we will explore the most common elements that make up an archetypal enterprise system and assemble them in a new and compelling way, reflecting the recursive patterns reflected in natural systems. Chapter 5 explores the archetypal management system at work. Chapters 6 through 12 break down each common management element and relate their importance and system interaction.

Part 3 begins the work of helping you diagnose your current system, analyze the potential changes, and design your EMS. Then we will look at the process of change management and how to affect change in the current system, and we will explore certain special cases such as technology, processes, innovation, and family businesses in light of the system. We will end with some final thoughts.

All along the way, stories and anecdotes from the field explain how a particular system concept or dynamic played out in real life, to make the concepts as practical and actionable as possible for enterprises of all sizes. The names of all companies and people involved have been changed to protect their anonymity. Many of these will be of particular interest for those working in and on family businesses, not-for-profits, and government agencies. Look for these paragraphs:

Note from the Field

These stories will help illuminate the power, beauty, and intrigue of systems. The names of the people and companies have been left off to protect the owners, managers, and families involved. Besides, the specifics don't matter. These notes are parables, designed to show you the system in action. Look at what these managers did in this situation. Don't do what this owner did.

Additionally, look for the following special notes about systems:

Behold: *Behold the System.* Systems are amazing constructs at which one often must marvel. These interludes will encourage and guide you to use the system's power and elegance to your advantage.

Beware: *Beware the System.* Systems have a mind and rhythm of their own and may often vex. Understanding how system dynamics invisibly and powerfully exert influence in and on your enterprise will help you to be more effective in managing within them.

Caution: This is not a how-to book with precise examples of management techniques you can cut and paste into your enterprise! While it is my sincere hope that you embrace the ideas herein and implement them in your enterprise, do not do so without first adapting them to your system, your circumstance, and your philosophy. Your enterprise, your system, is unique. Therefore, your management system must be unique to you, your philosophy, and your time and circumstance.

Chapter 1 on systems thinking contains a link where you can download a handy systems-thinking bookmark. Download it and use it to jog your memory as you proceed through the book and your journey. At the end of each chapter, you will find a list of takeaways from the chapter to lock in your learning.

Finally, as a point of reference, throughout the book I will use the term *enterprise* to connote the legal construct dedicated to a specific mission or purpose. This is distinct from the *organization*—that is, the physical construct and the associated people who do the work of the enterprise.

Acknowledgments

An army of mentors, friends, provocateurs, teachers, employees, and clients has contributed mightily to my journey, and therefore this book. I have worked for and with them, cried and laughed with them, succeeded and failed with them. I have heard their stories and walked their paths with them. They have carried me and I have carried them. While I owe them all an enormous debt of gratitude, there are simply too many to list, and all should and will remain anonymous.

Similarly, this book stands on the shoulders of great minds that have preceded me and have provided me with inspiration and building blocks. I have learned so much from the writings and guidance of countless great authors. I cite many of them throughout the book. I commend to you their writings, cited in the Notes and Recommended Reading sections. As you will learn in this book, you must form and articulate your own management system. The Enterprise Management System I describe was forged over the years with the help of these extraordinary mentors who did not know how strongly they influenced me. To all of them I owe an enormous thank you.

Serendipity played a huge role in my meeting my publisher. Had I planned my approach to publishing, I could not have chosen a better guide and mentor than David Hancock. From the instant I met David, I knew I was in the right hands. I would like to thank Bethany Marshall who made the introduction and stayed with me throughout the process. All of the people associated with Morgan James have made my journey to authorship among the most pleasant diversions I have embarked upon. I look forward to a long and fruitful relationship with them.

My editor, Amanda Rooker, has been invaluable in shaping *Simple_Complexity* and making it accessible and coherent. I cannot thank her enough. Also, a special shout out goes to my graphics muse and social media tour guide, Mitch Phillips, owner of DesignedbyMitch, whose graphics grace the pages of this book and whose steady hand shepherded me into the world of social media.

Finally, I owe a huge thank you to my family and friends for putting up with me during the process of writing *Simple_Complexity*. Special thanks to my lovely wife, Patricia, for her patience and editorial prowess.

Part 1

Systems Thinking:
The Unifying Discipline

Chapter 1

Introduction to Systems Thinking

Systems thinking [is] a way of thinking about, and a language for describing and understanding, the forces and interrelationships that shape the behavior of systems. This discipline helps us to see how to change systems more effectively, and to act more in tune with the natural processes of the natural and economic world . . . . It is the discipline that integrates the disciplines.
—Peter Senge[3]

In my years of consulting with companies of all sizes and types, I have commonly asked owners, managers, and board members if their company is a system. Invariably, they answer, "Yes, my company is a system." I then ask them if they have ever read about or studied systems thinking. The answer is almost invariably, "No." In my experience, most owners and managers have not heard of systems thinking, or do not believe that systems thinking has much to do with their business. They seem to grasp intuitively that their business is a system, but they have no language or models to guide their thinking.

The truth is your enterprise is a powerful system, and everything in it is intimately connected. Your enterprise structures and system dynamics *dominate* the behaviors of both the system as a whole and the employees in it. Systems thinking *is* the unifying discipline that will enable you to grasp the concept of your enterprise as a system. With time and attention most owners and managers have changed their thinking and believe that a systems-thinking approach is indispensable to managing their business enterprise.

System Defined

Since my task is to help you simplify your management thinking in an environment of noise and confusion, I use Donella Meadows's sparse, elegant, and powerful definition of a system:

> *A set of elements or parts that is coherently organized and interconnected in a pattern or structure that produces a characteristic set of behaviors, often classified as its function or purpose.*[4]

From Meadows's definition come the three essential components of a system:

✓ **Elements**
✓ **Interactions**
✓ **Purpose**

Let us discuss each component in more detail using a simple pocket watch as an example.

1. The **elements** of a system can be anything—people, time, money, resources, tools, and even other systems. One of the key practices in systems thinking is to be sure to identify all the elements in the system or subsystem (see discussion on boundaries) and the attributes the elements have or should have. For example, the system of a pocket watch is made of many fixed and moving parts.

2. What distinguishes a system from merely an assemblage of the elements is the **interactions** the elements engage in, by design or by happenstance, and the way those interactions shape the system dynamics. Once assembled the elements in sociotechnical systems take on a life, rhythms, and dynamics of their own. Sensing and understanding these rhythms and dynamics is essential to understanding the system. How do the parts of the pocket watch fit together and influence one another?

3. Finally, all human systems must have a **purpose**. If not, why bring the elements and interactions into play? Meadows suggests that *function* is more often utilized for inanimate systems and *purpose* for human systems. A pocket watch tells time, a function. The person wearing the

watch has somewhere to go, a purpose. Although some writers still refer to this as goal or function, I prefer to use, and I believe people respond best to, the term *purpose*.

The Importance of Purpose

I believe it is important to distinguish between the three terms—purpose, function, and goal—and I believe Meadows is correct to associate purpose with human systems. Your employees do not connect emotionally with functions or goals. They connect with purpose. Simon Sinek, in his illuminating work *Start with Why*, points out the critical need to connect with purpose, to answer the question why.[5]

As children, we constantly asked the question why, and we continue to do so as adults. We just stop asking it aloud. Your employees are constantly asking why, just not aloud. They want to know the answer to the question, "What's the purpose?" To perform at their best, they have to know the purpose of the system. You must provide the why. This distinct rationale for purpose will become clearer as you learn more about how purpose cascades through the organization.

Often owners and managers attempt to replace purpose with statements of vision, mission, objectives, and goals. This is a mistake. The system *will reveal* true purpose in spite of stated vision and mission statements or the absence thereof.

Beware: Your vision and mission statements must align with your purpose. The system will broadcast the real purpose regardless of stated vision or mission statements.

Note from the Field

A company constructed and adopted a vision to become a leader in its region, and a mission that included superior customer service, yet erected every conceivable barrier to fulfilling its stated purpose. The owner refused to invest in the needed infrastructure and capabilities to become a leader. Although customer service was part of the mission, there was no training for customer-facing employees, employees had no latitude to address customer issues at the time of service delivery, and refunds and returns were agonizingly hard for customers. Employees quickly came

> to understand that the real purpose of the company was not to become a leader through customer service, but to soldier on as in the past. The stated vision became a hollow promise and a source of cynicism.

Systems are always connected and always communicating. You know this from the "grapevine" in your company. The people in the system, your employees, will see, feel, or sense the real purpose. Your actions or lack thereof will reveal your real intent.

Conversely, many owners and managers deride these same statements as unnecessary or counterproductive. This is also a mistake. You will miss the power of connection, alignment, and guidance these documents provide. A system with a motivating purpose, a compelling vision and mission, and goals aligned with these is a powerful force.

Beware: Your vision and mission statements must reflect a worthy purpose. Bland, generic, or personal vision statements have no power to move employees.

Note from the Field

The owner of a very successful site-work and environmental remediation firm was a true self-made man, but gruff and direct. He had little use for frivolous pursuits, which he dubbed the creation of a vision and mission statement to be. As his son and daughter began to work in the business, they encouraged him to reconsider his position and write down his vision and mission. He finally relented and proposed to his assembled employees a vision of becoming a twenty million dollar company. The employees greeted the new vision with a silent, collective groan, and as the months passed performance actually dipped. This dip in performance convinced him of the futility of openly stating a vision. Working with the son and daughter, *we convinced him to make another attempt, but this time include the employees. After much discussion, the assembled team settled on becoming the premier site-work and environmental remediation firm in their region, a moving and compelling purpose. The owner could not believe the passion, enthusiasm, and pride the new vision unleashed. He remarked that the new collective vision reflected what he really wanted the firm to be, and his employees were more engaged than he had ever seen them. The firm easily met and surpassed his monetary goal and began to attract the top talent in the region. Such is the power of purpose.*

Finally, make sure your vision, mission, values, actions, and investments remain in alignment with your true purpose as you cascade them down the enterprise. Note: at different levels throughout the enterprise, you may switch from purpose to vision and mission to goals and objectives. This is fine as long as you are clear with all involved about what you mean by each of these terms. Language in the system is very important. It is critical to be precise, like a pocket watch, and to use consistent language and mental models.

Behold: The power comes when you align a moving, worthy human purpose with a clear and compelling vision that reflects that purpose and further aligns all the system components to serve that purpose.

Elements interact in order to achieve some **purpose**; seems simple enough, but how? Read on to see the *Simple_Complexity*.

Systems Thinking Tenets

[Systems thinking is] the reorientation of thought and world view ensuing from the introduction of "system" as a new scientific paradigm in contrast to the analytic, mechanistic, one-way causal paradigm of classic science.
—Ludwig von Bertalanffy[6]

Systems thinking is often referred to as a holistic way of thinking about systems, their dynamics, behaviors, and the environments in which they operate. From the great systems thinkers like Bertalanffy and the others cited in the Preface and listed in the Recommended Reading sections, certain basic system-thinking tenets have emerged. An understanding of these basic tenets will begin to reveal to you some of the powerful dynamics you may be sensing or feeling, but have been unable to pinpoint or articulate. As you read these tenets, keep in mind the admonition to both behold and beware the system. Each of these system tenets has powerful implications for management. Do not just read the words; envision the beauty and power of the concepts. I have provided some specific cautions as a reminder.

Helpful hint: Go to simplecomplexitybook.com to download a printable bookmark with the tenets. Print it out, laminate it, and use it as your bookmark as you read the remainder of the book to remind you of these key concepts.

1. *Interdependence of elements and their attributes.* The independent elements do not constitute a system, just as a pile of scattered watch parts do not make a watch or tell time. It is the bringing together of the elements for a particular purpose and the resulting interactions that constitute a system.

2. *Inputs and outputs.* The goal or purpose of the system usually manifests itself through the transformation of inputs into outputs—converting time, people, and money into goods and services. In an open system, such as an enterprise, inputs are admitted from the environment into the system. In short, there is a *flow* to systems.

3. *Goal seeking.* The interaction of the independent elements must result in some goal or purpose. As stated earlier a purpose or goal will arise from the interactions even if you have not provided one.
   Beware: Your employees will assume, rightly, that you have assembled them with the other elements for a purpose. In the absence of information to the contrary, they will assume a purpose for the enterprise.
   Behold: Connecting with employees around a shared purpose is powerful. If you have chosen well, your employees will want to engage in the purpose of the enterprise.

4. *Equifinality.* As you will see in this book, and have no doubt seen in your enterprise, there are many ways to use the assembled elements to achieve the purpose. There are alternative ways of attaining the same purpose. In systems talk we call this *convergence.*
   Behold: Properly used, this feature of systems can unleash tremendous creativity and innovation, deeply empowering the people in the system to find new ways forward.

5. *Multifinality.* It is possible using the same elements and interactions to attain alternative objectives (purposes) from the same inputs. In systems talk we call this *divergence.*

   Beware: Without real clarity of purpose and clear systemic guidance, the system can be, and often is, steered towards multiple competing purposes, or like a pocket watch that you neither clean nor wind periodically, the whole thing will just stop.

6. *Emergent properties.* Systems exhibit a powerful dynamic of creating properties that emerge from the system(s) that are not *elemental* and arise from the *interactions* and the *purpose.*

   Behold and Beware: Your corporate culture is an emergent property of your system. Culture is a powerful, undeniable component of your system that *will* be present in the system, yet one that you cannot address directly, because it *emerges* from the system.

7. *Self-organization.* Human systems exhibit the ability to self-organize, called *autopoiesis.* By bringing together the elements you set up a defined or implied purpose, and the system will begin to self-organize to accomplish that purpose.

   Behold: Similar to emergent properties, systems have the ability to structure themselves, to create new structure, to learn, to diversify, and to become more complex, to complexify.[7] In fact, your employees are already doing this. They will structure themselves how they see fit to accomplish the purpose, with or without your guidance. Properly used, this feature of systems can be very powerful and empowering.

   Beware: Improperly used, this feature of systems can be chaotic and disruptive. Conversely, being too restrictive in regards to this feature can make your enterprise feel like Gareth Morgan's "psychic prison"[8] a barren, forlorn, suffocating place, implacable in the face of changing circumstances.

8. *Unintended consequences.* The above two tenets, emergent properties and self-organization, often lead to unintended consequences. Systems have the powerful and vexing quality of striving towards the purpose often generating unintended consequences or unwanted results. This is precisely why you have to design your enterprise system and not let it evolve by default.

   Behold: Sometimes these unintended consequences are beneficial.

   Beware: Sometimes, they are detrimental. Management often lauds or blames individual employees for these consequences. As we will see in later chapters, most of the time these consequences are a direct result of the system—the *interaction* of the *elements* in response to the *purpose*. Rewarding or reprimanding individual employees for system-generated dynamics is usually counterproductive.

9. *Structure.* Having read the above features of systems, this tenet should be obvious. The structure of the system, intentional or self-organizational, often influences or dictates system behavior and the behavior of the participants in the system. For this reason, it is critical for you to examine the structure of your system and make sure all of your employees know and understand the structure and its implications.

10. *Boundaries.* There are no separate systems. Meadows writes, "In the real world boundaries don't exist. There are only boundaries of thought, perception, and social agreement—artificial, mental-model boundaries."[9] The system is always connected, never severable. We must establish boundaries to be able to manage the system, but these boundaries are fictitious, of our own making. This is another reason you must design your system, not let it emerge by default.

    Behold: This is true of your enterprise. There is no boundary between headquarters and the field, between engineering and marketing, between HR and accounting, and so on. All of these departments, functions, and people remain inexorably connected. We create boundaries in our minds to make sense of the system and to make it more manageable.

    Beware: However, the system itself does not recognize the boundary, only you do. Where to draw a boundary around and within a system depends on the purpose you wish to accomplish by defining such a boundary.

    Meadows continues, "Boundaries are of our own making, and they can and should be *reconsidered* for each new discussion, problem, or purpose."[10] There is no such thing as a fixed boundary.

11. *Viewpoint.* How you see the system, or part of the system, depends on your viewpoint, where you stand when you view and interact with the system (see discussion on the Möbius strip in the next section).

    Beware: You must remember that your viewpoint, or that of your employee, may be only a partial view of the system or system element. This is especially true when considered in conjunction with the artificial system boundaries you have established. If you believe all you see is all there is, you will be forever limited.

12. *Bounded rationality.* Bounded rationality, a term popularized by Herbert Simon,[11] refers to the natural, inevitable tendency for people within the system to behave as if the boundaries, which are artificially established and which we know are not real, are real. As soon as the boundaries are established, people will begin to maximize the interactions *within* the boundaries.

    Beware: The way each employee acts, driven by bounded rationality, may lead to decisions that further the purpose or welfare of the bounded subsystem element, but that are detrimental to the system as a whole. Things that happen inside the boundary influence things outside the boundary, and vice versa. For this reason, you must carefully consider incentives in light of the whole system.

13. *Differentiation.* The fictitious boundaries imposed on the system are there to create specialized units that perform specialized functions—marketing, finance, accounting, manufacturing, etc. This functional optimization is rational and necessary.

    Beware: You must constantly remind the people who lead and work in these functional areas, of their "systemicity," their inescapable connection to the larger system. There is no circumstance under which their actions are disconnected from the remainder of the system. Often these connections are unseen or misunderstood, leading to bounded rationality actions.

14. *Hierarchy.* Systems are complex wholes made up of smaller subsystems. These structures are naturally hierarchical. Remember that the structure of the system influences the dynamics and the behavior of the system. The fact that the system generates a hierarchy does not mean that the higher layers are more important than the lower layers. Yet this is exactly how many managers view the system (there is that viewpoint tenet again). All of the layers are equally important. The higher tiers of the structure exist only because the lower levels support and justify them.

15. *Recursive patterns.* System hierarchies are often comprised of simple recursive patterns. Your departmental structures with vice presidents, directors, managers, etc., cascading down through departments are an example of such a recursive pattern.

    Behold: Recursive patterns are comfortable precisely because they are familiar, but **beware**, perhaps the pattern should *not* persist.

16. *Feedback.* All systems require feedback loops that inform the system as to status, flows, and condition. Feedback is critical to the proper functioning of the system. You must exercise caution, however, as the real feedback that

is needed and actionable may not be the desired feedback and vice versa. Managers often try to shape or limit the feedback the employees see. This is usually a futile effort since participants in the system often see, or sense, the real feedback. Additionally, systems often hide critical feedback with delays, which mask real results and consequences.

17. *Delays.* System flow and throughput is often characterized by delays in information. Delays in feedback loops can mask important, often critical system information and system dynamics. Management must be aware of the delays.

Basic System Icon

As you can see from the systems-thinking tenets, systems are deceptively powerful constructs. They seem *simple* but are very *powerful*; not in direct ways but in very subtle and invisible ways. This is why you *must* use systems thinking to understand them. Once you have assembled the elements, those elements *will* start to interact and they *will* seek a purpose. For the purposes of this book, I use the Möbius strip (shown in Figure 1) as a powerful, suggestive, and iconic metaphor for a system and its subsystem parts and dynamics.

Figure 1. Classic Depiction of a Möbius Strip

The Möbius strip is the perfect metaphor for a system. It is *simple* yet *complex*, finite yet infinite, and bounded yet endless. A Möbius strip has the mathematical property of being nonorientable. You must orient yourself to it! How you see the strip depends on where you view it from, your *viewpoint.* What you see when you view the Möbius strip, your system, depends on your assumptions about the orientation, what you want to see, or what you have been trained to see. Just when you think you are oriented to which side of the strip you are on, the strip transports you to the other side. For these reasons, the Möbius strip is the perfect metaphor for a system. It is connected, continuous, and always communicating with the other elements of the system.

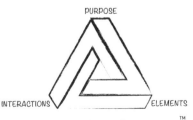

Figure 2. Basic System

I will use the idea of a Möbius strip to convey this opposing tension of simplicity and complexity. Rendering the basic system as a Möbius strip looks like Figure 2.

Here the three components of our system—elements, interactions, and purpose—are embodied in the Möbius strip.

As you can see, it is impossible to determine which component is the most important. It is impossible to separate the components. Therefore, you must orient yourself to the system rather than the other way around. You must understand the perspective from which you are viewing the system, your viewpoint.

Holism, Holons, Circles, and Loops

To understand fully systems thinking and to begin to see your management system through new and more powerful lenses requires refining your current thought processes with new techniques.

Holism

Systems thinking derives its power from the philosophic concept of holism. The theory of holism states the parts *cannot* exist independent of the whole. The parts are always intimately and inextricably connected one to the other and to the whole. As such, you cannot understand the parts without understanding the whole and must understand that the whole is greater than the sum of the parts. You must use a holistic approach to understanding and managing systems. You must expand your viewpoint and frame of reference. Simple problem solving and linear, cause-and-effect thinking are not sufficient. You must combat the reductionist tendency to look at your enterprise as a set of discrete parts to be optimized. Like the owner described in the Preface who had rigorously optimized the discrete components of her business yet still felt something was missing, you will have an incomplete picture of your enterprise if you do not look at it holistically and practice holism.

Hermeneutic Circle

The hermeneutic circle is a philosophic approach most often related to legal and religious texts.[12] Understanding a text hermeneutically requires you to practice reading and absorbing the text in a circular fashion. Completing the hermeneutic circle requires the reader to understand and have contextual reference of the whole in order to understand the parts while simultaneously having an understanding and contextual reference to the parts to understand the whole. You must travel through the full circle at least once to grasp the whole of the teaching. Repeated readings further refine your knowledge and grasp of the teachings. Your experience and biases influence your travel through the circle and should be examined and refined with each cycle.

You may get a sense of this by remembering when you were reading a book and you were only part way through. Even though you know some of the plot lines and characters, you may have only a vague idea of what the conclusion might be. Until you have completed the book, you are unsure. You have not completed the hermeneutic circle, so the parts are insufficient for you to complete the story. If you were to stop here, you would never know the whole story of the book. Once you have completed the book, the chapters, characters, and plot lines make sense. Each additional reading reveals more nuance and subtlety. Details you missed the first time emerge. You make connections that span the entire duration of the text.

Your enterprise is a complex text, a story, which you and your employees must understand holistically. You and they must travel the hermeneutic circle. To do this, you must have intimate knowledge of the whole *and* of the parts. Absent this understanding, competing purposes, viewpoints, and dynamics will inevitably erode performance. Remember, your system is perfectly designed to get the results it is getting today.

Holon

Arthur Koestler first promoted the concept of a holon in his book *The Ghost in the Machine.*[13] He concluded that in living organisms and social systems it appears easy to identify wholes and parts of wholes, but in fact, there are no such things. For instance, it appears easy to reduce your company to departments titled sales, manufacturing, accounting, etc., and suffer no ill consequence in doing so. However, this is not true. The parts and the whole are inextricable precisely because they constitute a system, which we know has no real boundaries. Koestler proposed the concept of a holon as a *mental* construct that exists simultaneously as a self-contained whole and a dependent part of the whole, as a means to describe the hybrid nature of system parts. Koestler's concept of a holon has powerful implications for managers. He writes that holons, while still being subject to direction and control from within the whole, can be autonomous and self-reliant and can act outside of such control.

Koestler's holon sounds a lot like a department, or an employee, or a process, even a policy or concept, does it not? Our departments, our employees, our processes and policies, etc., often appear to be independent and freestanding, but they are *always* a part of the system. You cannot forget this duality and you cannot let your employees forget it. Should you forget, bounded rationality is sure to creep into your thinking.

The power of the concept of a holon is that it forces you to remember the holistic nature of the system and all of its parts. A holon can be anything in the system, an element, a team, a process, an individual. It is a mental construct. The power in viewing the components as a holon comes from seeing the systemic nature of the component, in thinking holistically. You must begin to view these components of your enterprise system as holons that are both independent and dependent, both simple and complex.

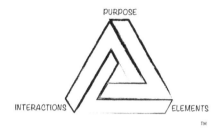

Figure 3. Basic Management System Holon

Koestler goes on to describe the ability of holons to self-organize (the concept of autopoiesis) into what he terms a *holarchy*.

Merging the description of a basic system and Koestler's concept of a holon, I will use the Möbius strip depiction of a basic system and *any* of its components as a holon (see Figure 3).

> **Behold:** The key, defining concept of systems thinking to remember is that *nothing* in the system is *ever* unconnected. This is the power of viewing the parts of your system as holons. A holon never loses its systemicity! Using the holon as a symbol should remind you to always consider the system implications.
>
> **Beware:** Your employee never ceases to be a part of and subject to the system. Your teams and departments can never be independent elements, free of system connections and dynamics. You should not optimize your processes with respect to fictitious boundaries, only as a part of the greater whole.

Your ideas and models of the system must reflect the holistic nature of the system. Remember that a key feature of a Möbius strip is that it is nonorientable. This is true of a holon. *You* must orient yourself to it. You must orient yourself to which side of the holon you are on, where the holon is in relation to all of the other system parts, where the holon resides in the holarchy, what dynamics emerge from the holon, and what inputs and outputs transit through the holon.

Let us look at an example of how to use the concept of a holon applied to a process. When viewing a process as a holon it is critical to identify the purpose of the process in light of both the local process environment, e.g. billing, and the greater system. If you only look at the local purpose, the process may end up being at cross-purposes to the greater enterprise purpose. You must trace all of the interactions the process may affect and all of the elements it may touch or influence.

Now let us look at the concept of a holon being applied to a management concept in your enterprise, such as leadership. There is a lot of management literature about leadership, yet how do we think about it in regards to the system? The holonic approach to this topic forces us to ask some fundamental questions about leadership as it relates to the system.

- What is the purpose of leadership in the system?
- Does leadership understand systems and practice systems thinking?
- Where do we need leadership in the system?
- How does leadership interact with the system and its components?
- What are the characteristics of a leader in this system?
- What should leadership interactions entail and look like?

Holons remind us that the component we are dealing with, whether it is a physical construct or a mental construct, is something that is *both* simple and complex.

Boyd's OODA Loop

Developed by United States Air Force Colonel John Boyd,[14] the phrase *OODA loop* refers to a simple yet powerful decision loop of *observe, orient, decide,* and *act*. Boyd developed the device initially as an iterative set of decision loops conducted by individual pilots and used in aerial combat. The pilot who cycles through more quickly and observes the environment more rigorously has a tactical advantage. Because these situations are constantly changing and new information is coming in, one must learn to go through the loops at a faster pace and reobserve the situation to reorient oneself to the new status. Boyd himself broadened the use and applicability beyond individual pilots to teams and organizations.

The OODA loop (shown in Figure 4) offers us a key technique for and insight into the need for orienting ourselves to the system and its holons. If we do not carefully observe the environment, our Möbius strip, we are at risk of *disorientation*. This is true of system holons. Managers and employees who do not become oriented to the holon and how it relates to other system holons and to the larger whole will be disoriented. They may misread the orientation of the holon, the dynamics of the holon, or both. Similarly, when we observe the system from our *viewpoint*, if we do not understand that the holon is inescapably tied to a system, our observation lens will not be in focus, leading to disorientation. We may begin to practice bounded rationality. Further, Boyd cautioned that we must be conscious of any biases, filters, or assumptions we have that influence our observation skills as we observe the holon. Therefore, Boyd's OODA loop is like the hermeneutic circle. We cannot get properly oriented to the system until we are oriented to the parts, but we cannot be oriented to the parts until we are oriented to the system. As managers, we must understand that our employees have to see these connections and loops or they too will become disoriented.

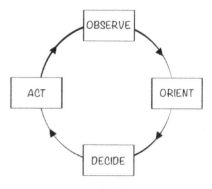

Therefore, what appears to be a simple, basic system has deep and profound implications and can appear

Figure 4. OODA Loop

to be overwhelmingly complex without the benefit of proper, systems-thinking context. As a manager, you must provide this context.

The Importance of Schema and Context

People see only what they are prepared to see.
—Ralph Waldo Emerson

A schema is a mental construct we develop as we engage in and interact with our social and physical environments. Jean Piaget in his pioneering work in cognitive development identified three primary schemata—behavioral, symbolic, and operational. We use each type to create "mental models" to explain and make sense of what we are experiencing, seeing, and thinking.[15] We are constantly revising and adding to our schemata using a process Piaget called assimilation and accommodation. We assimilate new experiences and concepts with our existing schema, or we accommodate and try to extend our schema to reflect our new understanding. However, if an idea or experience is too far outside of our ability to accommodate, this can lead to a retreat to our known, comfortable schema or a rejection of the new information.

You must understand that your employees are constantly developing and refining their schemata as they relate to your enterprise. They are looking for "the scheme" in your enterprise. You must help them see the systemic connections and develop schemata, mental models, which are consistent with your view of the system. These *shared mental models*[16] of the system provide the context for them to perform their function within the system. If you do not provide the context, they will attempt to complete the hermeneutic circle and make up their own schema.

Alan Kay, the legendary Xerox researcher, has said that the benefit of perspective and context adds 80 points to one's IQ.[17] Piaget[18] and Jon Medina explored the power of schema and context, and their importance to learning. Medina has reported the benefit of context can enhance learning and critical-thinking outcomes by 50–100 percent.[19] Giving a listener or learner context may double retention, comprehension, and accelerates learning. Understanding the context of new or additional information before absorbing the information is analogous to traveling through the hermeneutic circle. Having the context frames the whole and makes the parts easier to comprehend, and a better comprehension of the parts heightens the understanding of the whole.

When speaking to audiences, Medina often dramatically demonstrates the power of withholding or giving context.[20] He and a colleague do not give their audience context before they explain a *simple* task most everyone has completed hundreds of times. Even after repeated listening, the audience seldom has a clue as to the task Medina is describing. Some become frustrated and tune out. Some become amused and cease trying to comprehend. What appears to be an obscure, bewildering, and *complex* task utterly baffles the audience. When Medina and his colleague reveal that the task in question is the simple one of doing laundry, the audience is amazed. The context brings immediate recognition of the steps described in the process. When listening again, now heads nod with knowing confidence.

Think about how many times you have rushed through an explanation of what you want an employee or colleague to do. Did that employee have the needed context? Did you provide it? Did they understand the real purpose of the entreaty? If not, you may have unknowingly turned the simple into the complex *in their view*.

We will revisit this phenomenon and the need for providing context repeatedly in the remainder of *Simple_Complexity*. Remember, your system, represented by a Möbius strip, has the property of being nonorientable. We must orient ourselves to it and understand from which viewpoint we are seeing it.

Simplicity and Complexity

Complexity is a symptom of confusion, not a cause.
—Jeff Hawkins[21]

Progress is man's ability to complicate simplicity.
—Thor Heyerdahl[22]

Many management authors have described managing an enterprise as a series of dichotomies, often describing the tension between the polar ends of those dichotomies. One of the greatest of these is the tension between the simplicity of the individual tasks and functions within the enterprise and the complexity borne of the assemblage. The aggregation can seem like an impenetrable mess, and the management of it an overwhelming task.

Meadows writes that systems complexify; they self-evolve with their occupants into what can seem like unrecognizable messes.[23] Legendary systems theorist, Russell Ackoff says that as managers we do not solve problems, we manage these messes.[24] Many of the problems that confront managers do not have a simple solution. Systems seldom present easy solutions. Often in a system setting, we must, as Herbert Simon says, "satisfice."[25] We must split the difference between satisfying certain parts of the system and sacrificing certain parts. In a system, there will always be "winners" and "losers." As a manager, you must understand and embrace this duality.

Systems thinking helps you untangle the mess in your mind and develop a clear mental model of it.

Beware: Systems thinking does not make the mess go away. The mess remains, but you will be better able to understand and manage it.

Roger Martin in his wonderful book *The Opposable Mind,*[26] leadership scholar Nathan Harter,[27] and others encourage us to employ a "*both/and*" embrace of the dichotomy inherent in managing the system that is the enterprise. There is an emerging theory, proposed by several authors, called simplexity.[28] A combination of simplicity and complexity, simplexity theory suggests complexity and simplicity are complementary. The system is *both* simple *and* complex. As a manager, you must understand this duality and you must assist your employees in learning about and operating in this duality. There is no escaping the system with all of the inherent simplicity and complexity.

A similar dichotomy exists between simplicity and complexity of concepts. When you first learn how to operate a motor vehicle, there is so much to know that the process seems highly complex. Yet, today you can drive almost without thinking about it. Similarly, what is complex to some is simple to others. Often, your employees will view something as complex when it is merely hard or they do not understand it. Accounting is perceived to be hard when it is actually quite straightforward. The job of sales is often perceived to be complex when, in reality, it is difficult mentally and emotionally.

This is true with many complex adaptive systems such as an enterprise. The system appears to be bewilderingly complex. In reality, the system consists of many simple components. The complexity stems from the vast number of subsystems, elements, interactions, processes, and functions—from systems effects that are often emergent, nonobvious, and hidden from view. What appears to be objectively complex is often subjectively complex. If you know the subject, if you have the context, it seems less complex. You must learn it hermeneutically, parts and whole. Because your enterprise is a system, you must embrace systems thinking and teach it to your employees. If you do not you will deprive them of critical context, and they will be disoriented.

With context, enough knowledge, experience, and learning, the complex can become simple. However, Alfred North Whitehead offers a proper system caution:

> *The aim of science is to seek the simplest explanations of complex facts. We are apt to fall into the error of thinking that the facts are simple because simplicity is the goal of our quest. The guiding motto in the life of every natural philosopher should be, seek simplicity and distrust it.*[29]

Seek the simplicity of the system, and then do not trust it. Know that there is far more at work than the simple representation provided by a model or holon. Remember, no part of the system ever loses its systemicity. The simple rendering you are looking at is not that simple. As Alfred Korzybski said, "the map is not the territory."[30] Similarly George Box famously cautioned, "All models are wrong, some are useful."[31] Search for the most basic representation of all things and surface the underlying assumptions you have about them. Many things are simple in theory yet not easy. Their subtlety, holism, and adaptability are hard to grasp and make them appear complex. This is particularly true when assembled in large groups and patterns.

Additionally, the context or viewpoint from which you are seeing the thing or action or result is critical to understanding. The Möbius strip holon represents this dynamic perfectly and should remind you to follow Boyd's suggestion to stop and more deeply consider the situation, to *observe* again and *orient* yourself again.

Peter Senge in his seminal book about systems thinking, *The Fifth Discipline*, points out that every organization is full of learners and opportunities for learning, but what is lacking is a learning management system.[32] In my experience, most managers neglect to provide the systems context, which is a key component of such a management system; we neglect to complete the hermeneutic circle. The system as a whole and all of the occupants in it must learn. Read on to learn how to design such a system.

Behold: The system has its beauty, persistence, prevalence, and hidden powers, both simple and complex. However, **beware** the system for these same traits.

Key Takeaways
- ✓ The basic system components are—purpose, elements, and interactions.
- ✓ Everything is a system. You must adopt a holistic approach to analyzing and managing your enterprise.
- ✓ Beware and behold. You must remember the beauty of systems as well as their pervasive and invisible nature.
- ✓ Remember the hermeneutic circle. You cannot know the whole unless you know the parts, and you cannot know the parts unless you know the whole.
- ✓ The first two parts of Boyd's OODA loop—observe and orient—are the most important. Do not forget the importance of carefully observing, without prior biases and assumptions, and of becoming oriented. These two steps are the precursors to acting.
- ✓ Systems are both simple and complex.
- ✓ When in doubt, step back from the system and look at it from different viewpoints.

Recommended Reading for Chapter 1
Deming, W. Edwards. *The New Economics for Industry, Government, and Education.* Cambridge: MIT Press, 1993. Managers often relegate Deming's work to operations and statistical process control, but he was primarily a systems thinker. Early on, he argued for a holistic, systemic approach. However, in the old command-and-control order this was too much for most leaders to consider.

Drucker, Peter F. *The Essential Drucker.* New York: Harper, 2001. Drucker was and is a giant in management thought. Many managers have read his work, but have not seen how he infuses systems thinking throughout his texts.

Martin, Roger L. *The Opposable Mind: Winning Through Integrative Thinking.* Boston: Harvard Business School Press, 2009. A great primer on *both/and* thinking.

Meadows, Donella H. *Thinking in Systems*. White River Junction: Chelsea Green Publishing Company, 2008. Meadows provides a wonderful primer on systems thinking.

Senge, Peter M. *The Fifth Discipline*. New York: Doubleday, 1990. Senge is largely responsible for exposing more of the business world to systems thinking. Unfortunately, many managers think of his "learning organization" as the purview of human resources or a Chief Knowledge Officer, not that of the CEO, ignoring the holistic wisdom of his work.

Wheatley, Margaret J. *Leadership and the New Science: Discovering Order in a Chaotic World*. San Francisco: Berrett-Koehler Publishers, 2006. Wheatley subtly infuses the systems-thinking approach throughout this powerful book.

Chapter 2

The Enterprise as a System

Order always displays itself as patterns that develop over time.
—Margaret Wheatley

Systems reveal themselves as patterns, not as isolated incidents or data points.
—Fritjof Capra[33]

Now that you have a general understanding of systems, holism, and holons let us look at the enterprise as a system, actually a system of systems. In this chapter, we will explore the specific embodiment of a system as a sociotechnical enterprise. We will explore how the systems thinking tenets manifest themselves in your enterprise. Specifically, we will explore

1. How the system exhibits a recursive pattern in your enterprise.
2. How the tenets of hierarchy and self-organization manifest themselves in your enterprise.
3. The findings of Edwards Deming about systems results (throughput).
4. How bottlenecks and constraints affect throughput.
5. How systems reflect certain natural phenomena and how you can benefit from viewing your enterprise in light of these natural phenomena.

Remember our basic system holon, shown in Figure 5 on the next page.

This simple construct can represent the whole system and any one of its many parts or subsystems. Remember the key features of the system holon. It is always

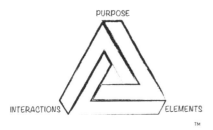

Figure 5. Basic System Holon

connected and communicating. You must acknowledge your viewpoint of it and become oriented to it repeatedly because it may have changed. The basic holon can be parsed into smaller holons—smaller systems. Conversely, you may merge holons into greater systems, for they are part of a system with no beginning or end.

Behold and Beware: The holons *are not* the answer or the one way you should think. They are diagnostic tools. They are the questions. They should spur you to ask questions about the particular part of your system you are considering. Are you properly oriented to the holon, to the system? Has the situation changed, and do you need to get reoriented? Are there boundaries or boundary conditions of which you need to be aware? Is your viewpoint affecting your understanding of the system? Are the elements the correct elements—are any missing? Is the purpose of the system or subsystem clear, and are the interactions healthy and appropriate?

A Recursive Pattern

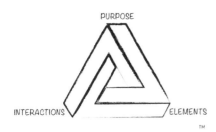

Figure 6. Team as a System Holon

Remember from the system tenets in Chapter 1 that systems often exhibit *recursive patterns* in their structure. The basic holon is such a construct. You can describe a team or department using the same basic pattern (shown in Figure 6).

Teams and departments represent a system with the same basic parts—elements and interactions with a clear need for purpose. You should regularly assess your teams and departments to make sure that the correct elements are in place, that the interactions are healthy and productive, and the purpose is clear. Similarly, the holon can represent a project within the enterprise (Figure 7).

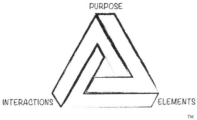

Figure 7. Project as a System Holon

A project is a special purpose team that takes on the characteristics of a system as soon as you assemble the elements of the project and give them a purpose. You should regularly assess the systemic nature and components of your projects. I believe you should treat every action in your enterprise as a project. A very useful exercise is to regularly assess those areas in your enterprise where you have assembled people and review the purpose and interactions.

Finally, an individual employee can be viewed as a system holon within your enterprise. An individual represents an element that has a purpose within the system and interacts with the greater system (Figure 8).

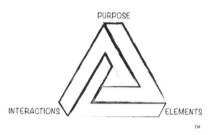

As you can see the simple, basic holon becomes a powerful building block of the enterprise, both *simple* and *complex*.

Figure 8. Individual as a System Holon

Viewed this way, people, teams, and projects become richer, more nuanced, and more far-reaching than when viewed simply as individuals or separate elements with clear boundaries. As holons, these elements are connected and are subject to all of the other system holons and dynamics. Using this metaphor yields a type of *both/and* thinking that is critical to thinking holistically about your enterprise. *Both* the individual *and* the system are important. *Both* the team *and* the system are the focus. Remember, the holons can never lose their systemicity. Systemicity becomes the key focus, not the individual or the team. This distinction will become more profound when we discuss the findings of W. Edwards Deming on failures, errors, mistakes, and misunderstandings within the system.

Hierarchy and Self-Organization

Using the basic holon we can begin to explore the enterprise holarchy as described by Koestler[34] (see the Chapter 1 discussion of holons). A key first insight from systems thinking that should drive your management thinking about the system is the important hierarchical linkage that plays out in the interaction of a superior holon with the purpose of the subordinate holon (see Figure 9).[35]

Management must be clear in this critical region. Clarity, transfer of purpose, and feedback during this interaction are some of the most important dynamics in the system. W. Edwards Deming wrote the following about this critical system dynamic.

It is management's job to direct the efforts of all components toward the aim of the system. The first step is clarification: everyone in the organization must understand the aim of the system, and how to direct his efforts toward it.[36]

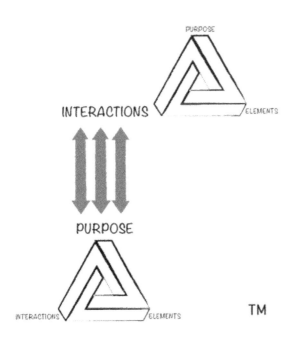

Figure 9. Critical Interaction: Transfer of Purpose to Subordinate Holon

Beware: The first, and perhaps most important, systems caution is, if you do not provide a purpose, or clarity about the purpose, your employees working in the system will make one up, or derive a purpose based on their beliefs or your actions. They will do this to traverse the hermeneutic circle in their mind and complete the story. Just as nature abhors a vacuum and will strive to fill it, systems *must* have a purpose and will provide their own if you do not give one or do not give it clearly.

A useful exercise is to take your current mission statement and organization chart and perform a quick audit. Ask yourself if you clearly understand the purpose of your enterprise or your part of the enterprise. Is it clear and compelling to you why you are doing what you are doing? Are there assumptions that are invisibly guiding the system? Is there alignment with the current reality? Answering the question why for all occupants of the system is critical to aligning purpose. A lack of clarity around the essential purpose of your organization will have catastrophic effects as that lack cascades down through the organization, providing many opportunities for *divergence* and *multifinality*.

Once you have reconciled your purpose, ask if you have been clear about that purpose with all those who report to you. Then ask yourself if they have clearly embraced the purpose and communicated it to their direct reports. You may be surprised at what you discover in this exercise. From this simple concept of transfer of purpose, it should be clear how dangerous even slight deviations in purpose become as they cascade down the organization. As we have discussed, systems exhibit the dynamics of self-organization and establishing hierarchy even in the absence of you doing so. In the absence of a clear and directed purpose, the level below will automatically establish a purpose and organize itself to satisfy that purpose.

Note from the Field

In some family businesses, the pride family members feel in the purpose of the firm can be very powerful and beneficial. However, purpose can be particularly vexing in some family businesses. Different purposes, held by different family members, can exist below the surface and cause unwanted tensions and dynamics. This is especially true in multigenerational businesses. Some family members will believe the enterprise exists to provide them with full employment or lifestyle, and others will believe in being market driven. Some members may want a liquidity event while others want to continue their involvement. The parents may want and pressure their offspring to join the business without reciprocal feelings. Families and family members at cross-purposes can lead to devastating consequences in the family unit outside of the enterprise. Family constitutions (see Chapter 16 for a description of family constitutions) can be particularly helpful by clarifying the purpose of the family business. The section on system tenets describing multifinality and equifinality may be helpful and particularly impactful for family members wrestling with this issue.

Behold: The basic system holon can be used as a diagnostic tool throughout the organization. A simple check of the basic system structure can reveal key insights and dynamics. Key questions to ask include "Are the purpose, elements, interactions, and boundary conditions clear to all in the holon and to those who interact with the holon?"

Replicating the recursive pattern down through the enterprise yields Koestler's holarchy (see Figure 10).

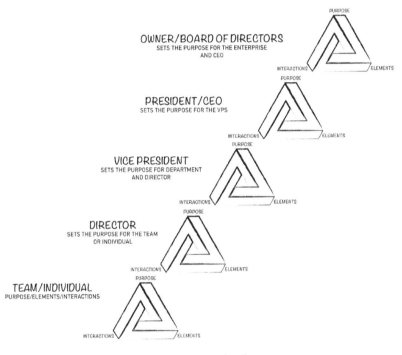

Figure 10. Holarchy

The holarchy can be extended to divisional structures as seen in Figure 11.

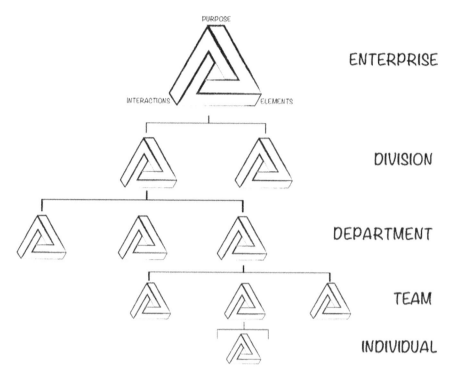

Figure 11. Divisional Holarchy

Similarly, as shown in Figure 12, the holarchy can represent the extended enterprise of customers, suppliers, and other stakeholders.

Figure 12. Extended Enterprise

Note in Figure 12 how the elements of one system in the extended enterprise align with the interactions of the system outside of your boundary. This is another example of the boundaryless nature of systems.

This simple mental model has powerful implications. First, it is imperative that you design and shape the interactions your enterprise has with the corresponding holons—vendors, or customers. Remember there are no real boundaries, so these interactions become critical components of your enterprise's success. Second, since systems are always connected and communicating, assuring the alignment of the purposes within the extended enterprise becomes crucial. This is particularly true of partnerships, joint ventures, and other similar legal constructs.

The importance of purpose, and clarity and consistency of purpose, throughout the organization cannot be overstated. However, in nature, and somewhat counterintuitively, hierarchical systems evolve from the bottom up, and the purpose of the upper layers is to serve the purposes of the lower layers and vice versa. As an example, let us look at an ocean reef. The original supporting structure of the reef existed before the current living, interacting top layer and serves to support the living layer and anchor it to the seabed. The living layer exists only of the foregoing, now passive, structure, but serves the structure by remaining alive and vibrant. If the living layer dies, the reef ceases to perform its function and the whole structure is at risk.

Often as managers, we forget this important system dynamic. Remember the system tenet of viewpoint tells us that where we view the system from affects our perception of it. We view and manage the organization from the top down. We set the purpose from the top down. However, remember that from a natural systems perspective, the upper layers serve the lower levels and vice versa. Sales people in the field, service representatives, assemblers on the plant floor, and relief workers in a camp are the front line of the enterprise where the real work is accomplished. The upper levels exist to serve the lower levels. Start-ups go from founder to team to functional departments to divisions to multidivisional corporations—they *complexify*. The basic holarchy is built from the bottom up. We see this pattern repeatedly, yet due to time delays or the fact that we are new to the organization, we forget the lesson. The later layers exist to assist the earlier constructs.

Max De Pree offers wonderful guidance here. He writes "hierarchy and equality are not mutually exclusive. Hierarchy provides connections. Equality makes hierarchy responsive and responsible."[37]

Beware: Most managers do not view an enterprise this way. The hierarchy is often established long before we, the managers arrive, and the only view we have of the system is through the lens of transferring purpose down through the system holarchy. We do not recognize the importance and the power of the subordinate system layers and the real purpose of the layer they reside in. As a manager, you must understand this key system dynamic and manage accordingly.

Findings of W. Edwards Deming

W. Edwards Deming, one of the titans of management literature, reported that in his experience upwards of 94 percent of all errors, defects, and mistakes were systemic.[38] He reported that the people in the enterprise, in the system, want to do the right thing (if not, you hired the wrong people or they are not following your company's values), but the system drove them to do the wrong, or contrary, or inefficient thing. Deming writes:

> *The appreciation of a system involves understanding how interactions between the elements of a system can result in internal restrictions that force the system to behave as a single organism that automatically seeks a steady state. This steady state determines the output of the system rather than the individual elements. Thus it is the structure of the organization rather than the employees, alone, which holds the key to improving the quality of output.*[39]

We see in this passage the concepts of an *interconnected system* (single organism) and *bounded rationality* (internal restrictions). It is for this reason that viewing the employees and teams as holons is so powerful. Realizing that the individual employees want to do the right thing but, often, are forced by the system into the wrong behavior has profound managerial implications. Here we see clearly the need for *both/and* thinking. It is crucial to evaluate *both* the individual *and* the system for performance. They are not severable. The linkages are inextricable.

Deming believed that most, if not all, traditional reward, recognition, and advancement systems were ill advised and in many cases counterproductive. There is significant research that indicates this is so. Alfie Kohn,[40] in his book *Punished by Rewards,* and Daniel Pink,[41] in his book *Drive,* both write extensively about the damage of misplaced and misunderstood incentives. Deming, Kohn, and Pink all caution against the implementation of rewards for individual performance in a system setting. Incentives must take into account the systemic and behavioral effects that may occur. This is particularly true in light of the system concept of bounded rationality where actors in the system will act to optimize their particular part of the system (called point or local optimization), often at the expense of the larger system.

Note from the Field

A professor at a major research institution is well respected in his field and beloved by his students and alumni. He has achieved tenure and a senior role on the faculty. He would prefer to spend his time teaching and interacting with students and industry in practical applications. Yet his institution requires him to pursue grants and advanced research, and these activities have essentially removed him from the classroom. His heart is not in these efforts. He pursues them only because it is the expectation of the system. Conversely, a new faculty member sought out this university precisely for the research it conducts. She finds teaching tedious and students a necessary distraction. She would much prefer to research full-time and not teach. Yet the system requires her to teach. Why not reverse the roles? The answer is because the system is not designed that way. Over the years, systems and processes have developed and emerged, and they have diverged. The needs of the university, the academy, the individual faculty members, and the students are at cross-purposes. The system forces each occupant into a form of suboptimization. All of the elements of the system are intelligent and well meaning, but the system causes certain behaviors. The system still works, in fact works relatively well, but behavior is shaped by the system. This is a key insight for management.

Optimization, Suboptimization, and Throughput

Remember that your enterprise is a system designed to convert inputs into outputs, a term we call *throughput*. The goal is to optimize total system throughput—e.g., to get the highest possible output (in quantity, quality, or some combination) from the chosen inputs. Optimization must occur at the system level, at the *enterprise* level. You should only undertake optimization at specific points in the system after carefully assessing the impact on *total system throughput*.

Unfortunately, most managers and companies, acting according to bounded rationality, try to optimize every *individual* node, function, process, or holon within the system. This is often counterproductive and occasionally disastrous. Since a company is a *system* and *interconnected*, every action to optimize or change one node, by definition, sends a wave through the rest of the system nodes. Some of the consequences are favorable, but often, unintended consequences wreak havoc in other nodes of the system well away from the origin and long removed in time.

Note from the Field

The CEO of a family enterprise is concerned about cash flow. She mentions her concerns to her controller. Because of this casual remark, the controller takes action to speed up cash flow and improve collections by instituting a more aggressive collections policy. The controller instructs his staff to restrict credit, accelerate collections, and push nonconforming accounts to collections faster. These changes happen quickly in accounts receivable as the controller's staff dutifully implement the optimization effort. However, the effects are not felt for some time as new orders and existing invoices come up for review due to a delay in the feedback loop. Over time, the customer companies' purchasing and accounts payable departments come to dislike the changes. At a meeting, the CFO of one customer company informs her management that the supplier (our CEOs company) is "hard to work with." The operations head chimes in and agrees. Consequently, the customer's management tells the head of supply chain to find a more agreeable supplier. Predictably, sales decline at our CEO's company but only after time has elapsed. Seeing the decline in sales, our intrepid CEO instructs the sales manager to "light a fire" under sales and to drive the sales staff harder because it is obvious that they are slacking off, a fact proven by the declining sales.

The problem is point optimization of a small part of the system. Point or local optimization is often counterproductive, the time lag in the system hides the root cause, and the result is suboptimal total system throughput.

You must optimize the *system*, which usually entails *suboptimizing* one or more points in the system. This is highly counterintuitive and is at odds with much of the management advice dispensed, in fact with how management is taught. Much of that advice concentrates on optimizing a subsystem of the enterprise system—leadership, planning, processes, etc. All of this advice is very helpful, but *only* in the context of viewing the actions as a part of the total enterprise system of systems. Also counterintuitive is the notion that while an individual holon may react in a linear cause-and-effect way, a system of systems usually does not. As owners, executive directors, and senior managers, you have the broadest knowledge of the enterprise and the greatest ability to affect change throughout the organization. You must be the enterprise system diagnosticians and engineers.

Bottlenecks and the Theory of Constraints

Eliyahu M. Goldratt[42] in his wonderful book *The Goal* writes extensively and compellingly about the theory of constraints. Theory of constraints is a methodology for thinking about and solving system throughput problems. There will always be certain parts of the system that *limit* the total system throughput. Goldratt calls these points, *bottlenecks*. No amount of point optimization before or after the bottleneck will improve total system throughput as long as the bottleneck remains the limiting factor. As an example, say a homebuilder only had one framing crew, but multiple crews for foundations, roofing, and trim. The constraint, the bottleneck, to her throughput would be framing. No matter how many roofing crews she has, the limited number of framing crews constrains her ability to finish houses.

To increase system throughput one must relieve the bottleneck. However, since there will *always* be a constraining part of the system, the bottleneck will merely migrate to another part of the system. Managers must be aware of these system dynamics. Using the holistic approach, you must try to predict where the bottleneck will migrate and what the ensuing consequences will be. The methodology consists of the following steps:

- ✓ Find where the *system* is constrained (i.e. bottleneck).
- ✓ Understand the constraint, develop a solution, predict second-order system effects and determine if you can live with those.
- ✓ Implement the proposed solution.
- ✓ Look for where bottleneck migrated (i.e. new constraint in system).

In this regard, theory of constraints is similar to the Plan, Do, Check, Act (PDCA) cycle from total quality management and continuous improvement.[43] Goldratt concludes with three questions for leaders:

- ✓ What to change?
- ✓ What to change to?
- ✓ How to cause the change?

As we will discuss in the next chapter and in Chapter 14, "Change and the System," you must become comfortable constantly changing the system to remain in alignment with the new reality.

Beware: Managers often lose sight of the fact that they are *always* dealing with a system. They begin changing things from a viewpoint bounded by what they see, bounded rationality. You must always realize that any change will inevitably have consequences somewhere else in the system. It has to. It is all connected.

Behold: Our new way of viewing the enterprise, as an assemblage of holons with *both/and* thinking becomes a powerful diagnostic tool for assessing system throughput and optimization.

Senge's Learning Organization

Peter Senge in his work *The Fifth Discipline* writes that the most important management discipline is systems thinking.[44] He argues, as I do, that you must understand you are living and managing in a system. You must have an understanding of system dynamics, and you must have a common language and tools to teach systems thinking throughout the enterprise.

Similar to Deming, Senge points out that most, if not all, organizations are populated with employees who want to do the right thing and want to learn, but he notes that merely having people in the system who want to learn is insufficient. Your employees must interact in a *learning management system*. Your people, who operate within the system, must be aware of the system's power and reach. They must have a common way to talk about the system and common views of it (remember the viewpoint tenet of systems thinking). As we discussed in Chapter 1, your employees will be constantly developing and refining their schemata to understand what they are experiencing within the system.

Senge calls these views "mental models." We all have powerful assumptions that drive us to construct powerful mental models of the system in which we operate. If we have differing assumptions and mental models of the same system, disorientation is bound to occur. Similarly, disorientation occurs when participants in the system create their own mental models based on observations made using nonsystem lenses and practicing bounded rationality. As systems thinkers, we know they will do this. Absent clear input on the system from management, participants in a system will make up their own mental models of, and assumptions about, the system. They have to in order to complete the OODA loop in their mind, to travel around the hermeneutic circle and understand the story.

You must ensure that the language and mental models are clear, consistent, and appropriate to the purpose, elements, and interactions. However, that learning must take place from the bottom up. You cannot force learning. Your employees have to learn for themselves and you must provide the environment for them to do so: Senge's "learning organization."

Note from the Field

At the request of a board member, I was working with the senior management team of a new client. I was talking to them about the power of systems thinking and the concept of mental models, and they provided this cautionary tale about conflicting mental models. The board member told me one of the areas they were struggling with as an organization was project management. I asked the assembled senior management team about this perception. As a Vice President explained the problems with project management, the COO chimed in that it was a problem with program management. Another VP said project management and program management were the same thing. This brought a storm of disagreement. I stopped the discussion and asked each one of the assembled senior managers to write down their assumptions and mental models of project or program management at the firm. The results were revealing. All seven of the individuals had a different viewpoint, and a different mental model, of project/program management in the company. Some believed they were one in the same. Some believed one or the other was superior. Some believed that the process included account management, and some did not. Some believed the process included budget reporting and responsibility, and some did not. Some believed there was only one level of project management, and others believed there were several levels. Little wonder this company was struggling with project management! If the senior management, from the CEO down, had seven different mental models with differing language and definitions for project management, imagine how confused the staff must have been. Imagine the frustration and inefficiency.

Within the system, common language and common mental models must be the norm. The organization must learn these, not just each individual. Similar to the hermeneutic circle the whole organization must learn the parts, and the parts must learn the whole. Senge wrote extensively about this need in learning systems. If you have chosen your employees well, they will want to learn. They will want to learn individually, but they must also learn the system. Then the whole must learn, must become a learning organization. Senge found that all learning organizations have these elements:

- ✓ **Systems thinking.** The organization must practice systems thinking and harmonize around the shared systems.
- ✓ **Personal mastery.** Individuals must master their own function, their part of the system, and, most importantly, develop the ability to view both objectively, connecting their personal vision with that of the system.
- ✓ **Common mental models.** All participants must have common mental models of shared processes and activities based on shared assumptions.
- ✓ **Building a shared vision.** The purposes of the organization must be aligned to a shared vision up and down the organization. They cannot be working at "cross-purposes."
- ✓ **Team learning.** Teams need to have the ability to learn as a team and in a team setting.

Brownian Motion

In addition to Senge, many other management thinkers have looked to natural system phenomena as a means to understanding management. Margaret Wheatley, in her illuminating book *Leadership and the New Science,* proposes that organizations are like quantum physics constructs—constantly communicating bundles of energy and information akin to fields.[45] This metaphor has powerful implications for managers and leads to the exploration of two final concepts concerning systems. Both are from the natural sciences.

Brownian motion, also called Brownian movement, refers to the physical phenomena in which some quantity of elements is constantly undergoing small, random fluctuations around each element. The phenomenon is named for the Scottish botanist Robert Brown, who was the first to study such fluctuations (1827). Brown noted that, if a medium contains a number of particles and there is no preferred direction (think purpose and shared vision) just the random oscillations, over time the particles will tend to spread evenly throughout the medium and achieve a form of stasis or static equilibrium. Brownian motion is then defined as *the continuous haphazard movement of particles of matter suspended in a liquid or gas.* Brown referred to the forces active on the particles as unbalanced forces.

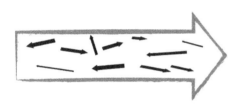

Figure 13. Aligning the Arrows—Before

Brownian motion offers a powerful image of organizations subject to unbalanced forces and misaligned purposes. Viewing an enterprise through the lens of Brownian motion looks like Figure 13.

If elements of your Enterprise Management System are unbalanced or misaligned, "at cross-purposes," chances are those effects are influencing other system elements in some way. Remember, it is all connected and your organization is perfectly designed to get the results it is getting today. Just from the visualization, one can deduce such an organization would struggle with throughput and communication, and perhaps, cultural issues.

I propose a derivative version of Brownian motion applied to organizations—Enterprise Brownian Motion (EBM). Enterprise Brownian Motion is the continuous haphazard movement of subsystems and/or individual people working in the enterprise due to well-intentioned management employing bounded rationality trying to point-optimize a system of systems.

These unbalanced forces (point optimization) act on the organization to slow it down, defocus it, and continually push it in unintended directions. This leads to wasted time, money, energy, and saps productivity, throughput, and employee satisfaction.

Entropy

Entropy is similar to Brownian motion and is the amount of disorder or randomness present in any system. The result of entropy and Brownian motion looks something like Figure 13. Individual holons are misaligned due to unclear system dynamics—lack of clear purpose, inappropriate interactions, dysfunctional elements, inappropriate incentives, bounded rationality, etc. The result is a chaotic force field where miscommunications and frustrating stasis abound. Many managers tell me their organization looks exactly like this.

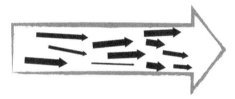

Your job as a leader and manager is to reduce entropy and combat Enterprise Brownian Motion. You are the system architect and engineer who can see and sense these dynamics.

Figure 14. Aligning the Arrows—After

Your goal, and the goal of your Enterprise Management System, is to align the forces and energies as shown in Figure 14.

Each energy field, each holon, is generally aligned with the direction of the whole, and each one is more focused and powerful in delivering its energy to the system.

However, how do we get there? Let us go back to the basic system holon. As we see in Figure 15, by slightly rotating the holon, we can give it a clear sense of direction derived from its purpose.

INTERACTIONS

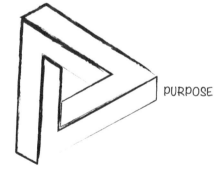

PURPOSE

ELEMENTS

Figure 15. New Orientation for Basic Holon

By extending the Möbius strip, we convert the basic system into a force field with amplitude and direction. You will remember that a basic system tenet is that social systems are open to inputs from the outside. These are your new entrants, the new employees you bring into your system for growth. The system at the enterprise level looks like Figure 16:

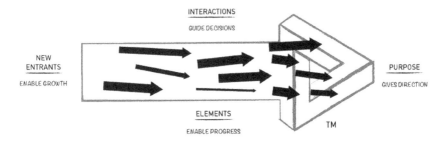

Figure 16. EMS with System Components

Your Enterprise Management System harnesses all of the energy and information of the holons by aligning it and focusing it on the purpose. The Enterprise Management System strives to *optimize* the *throughput* of the organization to maximize the use of the only three resources we control:

✓ *People.* The most important asset.
✓ *Money.* The efficient use of which will be the measure of management's success.
✓ *Time.* The most volatile and fleeting resource.

Replacing the individual energy fields with systems holons yields Figure 17, or a system-of-systems view.

This simple graphic representation demonstrates how important each element and holon is when looked at in light of the theory of constraints, entropy, and Brownian motion.

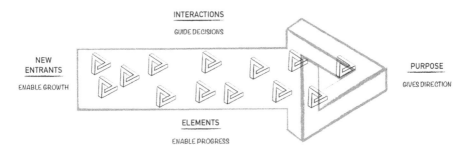

Figure 17. The System of Systems with Teams and Individuals

Key Takeaways

✓ An enterprise is formed from recursive patterns of the basic holon.

✓ The holons are *both* simple *and* complex, so you must practice *both/and* thinking.

✓ People, teams, and projects are holons of energy and information that are constantly interacting in pursuit of the system's purpose.

✓ Think in terms of holarchy not hierarchy—levels within the system are just structural differences not entitlements.

✓ The holons are the questions not the answers—diagnostic tools, not dictates.

✓ Total system throughput is the key management goal, not local or point optimization. Beware bounded rationality.

✓ There will always be a system bottleneck. Local optimization around it is usually wasted effort and may be counterproductive.

✓ If you have hired the right people, they will want to do the right thing; check the people *and* the system.

✓ Your job is to minimize entropy and Brownian motion.

Recommended Reading for Chapter 2

Deming, W. Edwards. *Out of the Crisis*. Cambridge: MIT Press, 1982.

Drucker, Peter F. *The Essential Drucker*. New York: Harper, 2001.

Goldratt, Eliyahu M. *The Goal: A Process of Ongoing Improvement*. Great Barrington: North River Press, 1984. *The Goal* is very engaging and reads like a novel. Beware: Do not be fooled into thinking it is not serious. It is a wonderful and powerful management book.

Meadows, Donella H. *Thinking in Systems*. White River Junction: Chelsea Green Publishing Company, 2008.

Senge, Peter M. *The Fifth Discipline*. New York: Doubleday, 1990.

Wheatley, Margaret J. *Leadership and the New Science: Discovering Order in a Chaotic World*. San Francisco: Berrett-Koehler Publishers, 2006.

Chapter 3

The Genesis of Your System

The beginning is the most important part of the work.
—Plato[46]

Years ago, I was in a management course and the professor proclaimed, "A company represents an *n* dimensional problem," using *n* as a variable for which we could substitute any number. When we asked him what a good number for *n* was, he stammered and said, "Any number you want." When asked if one was sufficient he said, "No." Another student asked, "How about 100?" "Maybe," came the reply. "So how many dimensions are there?" a student asked. "I don't know, perhaps an infinite number" was the answer. I must admit this exchange did not engender much confidence in me at the time. I wanted a definitive answer. I wanted a definitive number of variables; assembled in a simple, clear model.

I have now learned there is not one definitive equation or set of equations. There are a seemingly infinite number of variables to a business and many models to describe it. That is the point. You must become comfortable with the inherent lack of precision. You must embrace the ambiguity of not knowing the exact answer. There is not one definitive way to run a company. Your company is a living, breathing system that changes every day. You must learn to observe your system and to sense its rhythms.

As managers, we all use simple models, schema, as proxies and metaphors to represent more complex and nuanced concepts. However, as Peter Senge and others have pointed out, often we do not have a simple set of models,

42

a clear view, of the very complex enterprise we are managing, the enterprise model. I hope the holon and holarchic models I showed you in Chapter 1 have provided you with a start and some context. Next, I will be introducing you to some additional models of the enterprise and its dynamics based on systems thinking. The models I share should spur deep thought about the management system you use to manage your enterprise. You may not even be aware that you are subject to the dynamics represented by the models. The models will give you new perspective and context concerning the company you manage, your enterprise.

Peter Drucker provided some of the most profound context for the formation and prosecution of an enterprise with his *The Theory of the Business*.[47] In this simple but powerful treatise, Drucker provides clarity and context for how your *current* management system (remember you have one by default or by design) came into being at its genesis, and how it continues to come into being.

Drucker's theory proposes there are three key sets of assumptions made that brought your enterprise to life and shape it today:

1. At some time you, or your predecessors, made assumptions about the *environment* in which the enterprise exists—assumptions about the society, markets, customers, technology, and other factors that drive your business and are the elements of a classic, strategic situation analysis.

2. From the assumption about the environment, assumptions were made about the *purpose*, or mission, of the enterprise—assumptions about why your enterprise exists. A vision of what value the enterprise brings to the market; a clear sense of what your enterprise is designed to do.

3. Finally, the assumptions about your mission drive assumptions about the *systems*, *skills*, and *competencies* needed by the enterprise to accomplish that mission. Assumptions based on answers to questions such as, Where must we be excellent? What processes must be in place? Whom shall we hire?

You will note from the model of Drucker's theory that fundamental assumptions about our enterprise shape everything. These assumptions provide the context for your enterprise. They shape your purpose and the resulting system. Yet, many of these assumptions were made years ago or have survived unchallenged and without regard to veracity. In many companies, the fundamental assumptions are unknown to the vast majority of the occupants, they are *invisible*, and they have gone unexamined for years.

Invisible Assumptions

I will give you a ridiculous example of just one these invisible assumptions. Every business in the world is operating under the unstated assumption that the sun will rise the next morning. If this assumption were not true, most owners would be doing something other than counting the day's receipts or preparing for their next meeting. It is a useful assumption. We have 4,000 years of recorded history that tells us it is sound to assume this. However, what other assumptions are you making about the environment your enterprise resides in, your reality?

What assumptions have you made or are you making about

- ✓ Your markets?
- ✓ Your market segments?
- ✓ Your customers and their needs and buying behaviors?
- ✓ Your needed skills and competencies?
- ✓ Others?

Note from the Field

An example of an unexamined assumption is revealed in a family business. As a new fourth generation moved into management, the young son who had been named CEO asked for help to assemble an outside board. As the new board reviewed the existing financial results and the plans and strategies of the many divisions and businesses that made up the enterprise, it discovered a division that was performing very badly. The board asked about how it had been performing in the recent past. In unison, the family members admitted that the business in question had been losing money for years. In fact, they admitted that they were not very good at the business and did not particularly like the business. Digging deeper into this curious reality, it became clear the successive generations assumed they had to stay in the business because the grandfather started the whole company with that business. While many of the family members had questioned *the reasons for staying in the business and complained about the results, they never addressed the underlying assumption.*

As you know from Chapter 1, these assumptions *must* be in place. Your employees, occupants of the system, will make up assumptions about the system to reconcile their experience with it. They have to do this to complete their schemata and to travel the hermeneutic circle. They know they are in a system and they see it operate, so they *assume* you planned the particular operation or support the behavior. Oftentimes, as the above example shows, nothing could be further from the truth.

Graphically, my model of Drucker's theory looks like Figure 18.

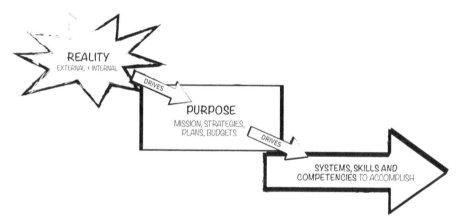

Figure 18. Graphic of Theory of the Business

Embedded in this simple model are three very profound implications that you must understand.

1. Your *entire enterprise rests on a foundation of assumptions.* Your enterprise, its systems, attendant skills, and competencies are, or were, created in response to the environment you are in and decisions about your mission in light of that environment.

2. Your Enterprise Management System, subsystems, processes, and competencies are following artifacts of the assumptions you made in assessing the environment and coalescing around a purpose or mission.

3. As a result, you must align your purpose and systems with your reality, and you must constantly revisit and renew the theory of your business to stay in alignment with the current reality.

This simple representation provides powerful insight into key management thought and the entreaties of so many management consultants and books (see Recommended Reading sections). It highlights the importance of strategic planning with rigorous analysis of the external environment as proposed by Porter, Bartlett and Ghoshal, Prahalad, and others. It stresses the importance of leadership for divining the purpose of the enterprise and aligning the enterprise with the purpose, vision, mission, etc., as proposed by Collins, Porras, Bennis, Maxwell, and others. It clearly shows the important linking role planning and leadership play in execution as cited by Welch, Bossidy and Charan, and others. It illuminates how important it is to align enterprise processes and competencies with these realities and purpose as proposed by Drucker, Hammer, Champy, and others. Finally, since the reality is constantly changing it implies the importance of change management as a key management skill.

A very useful technique is to begin to surface the assumptions that underlie your enterprise and actually write them down in simple terms. Discuss them with your management team. See if there is agreement on these powerful, invisible drivers of enterprise dynamics. You may be surprised at what you find. It is critical that you surface these assumptions and examine the impact they have on your enterprise.

The Management Paradox

My simple model of Drucker's theory also leads directly to the grand management paradox. Your charge as a manager is to make the system predictable and repeatable. It is a worthy goal and one for which you must always strive. Cruelly, it is a fool's errand, because you will never finish the task and the environment for which you are designing the system is always changing. That is the paradox. In some industries, this change is lightning fast, with changes visited upon the enterprise at dizzying speed and with relentless consequence. In others, the slow pace of change is comforting, but deceptive. The slow pace allows you to believe your environment is stable. Thinking back on our discussion about assumptions, is this a good assumption to make?

The word *management* derives from the Italian word *maneggiare* used to denote handling and training (originally of horses), which is itself a derivative of the Latin word for hand: *manus*. The bulk of management texts, guidance, and teaching are designed to make our actions and processes predictable and repeatable. We parse the enterprise into "manageable" divisions and then manage them to make them conform to our will. We want to handle them, to tame them.

This behavior is necessary and admirable. However, it can and often does lead to the enterprise becoming static and resistant to change. This fixation, and the desire of managers to make the resulting enterprise predictable and repeatable, often leads to a form of enterprise *stasis*, a static equilibrium that is very hard to change. Your systems, skills, competencies, and the culture that binds them together, all begin to ossify and become resistant to necessary changes implied by the reality in which the enterprise resides. The enterprise bogs down, mired in a static equilibrium from which it is hard to escape. In her illuminating book *How Institutions Think*, Mary Douglas provides a powerful clarion call to managers and leaders regarding this stasis:

> *Institutions systematically direct individual memory and channel our perceptions into forms compatible with the relations they authorize. They fix processes that are essentially dynamic, they hide their influence, and they rouse our emotions to a standardized pitch on standardized issues. Add to all this that they endow themselves with rightness and send their mutual corroboration cascading through all levels of our information system.*[48]

In such an enterprise, change efforts are resisted, new ideas and methods embattled. Paradoxically, this stasis feels safe and comfortable when in fact the reality may be changing to where the status quo is the *most* dangerous course of action. An organization trapped in this type of static equilibrium is very hard to move and to change. The natural tendency is to revert to the status quo as depicted in Figure 19.

The management paradox you face is, the enterprise you are managing was founded on assumptions derived

Figure 19. Static Equilibrium— Resistance to Change

from the environment, and that environment is ever changing. Your reality is constantly changing, both outside and inside the enterprise. Outside the enterprise markets, customer needs, economic factors, and a host of variables are constantly shifting. Similarly, inside the enterprise, employees, systems, and processes are, or perhaps should be, shifting, growing, declining, and retiring. Yet the elements of purpose, the vision and mission of the enterprise, often remain fixed. Only grudgingly does the fundamental purpose of the enterprise change.

When viewed graphically, Drucker's theory illuminates the need to establish not a *static* equilibrium but a *dynamic* equilibrium between the current state of the enterprise system and the reality it resides in, pivoting upon its purpose and the resulting mission and plans.

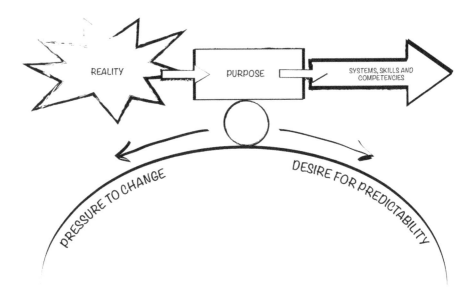

Figure 20. Dynamic Equilibrium: Poised to Change

Figure 20 dramatically reveals the grand paradox—you must prepare the enterprise for constant change while simultaneously working to perfect the workings of a living breathing system. Preparing an enterprise for change requires the occupants to be aware of all of the dynamics, internal and external, that drive the need for change. Mary Douglas continues her entreaty, "The first step in resistance is to discover how the institutional grip is laid upon our mind."[49]

Leadership and the occupants of the system must clearly see the need to change. For the enterprise to remain relevant and for change to occur, Todd Jick of Harvard says that leadership must endeavor to get every occupant of the system as uncomfortable with the status quo as leadership has become.[50] Only when the whole of the organization sees the need for change will change be possible.

However, even this visibility does not guarantee that any change will occur. Leading an organization that rests on a knife-edge is inherently dangerous. As you can see from Figure 20, an enterprise so positioned can easily escape the equilibrium in the wrong direction. A nudge one way or the other can create a snowball effect sending the enterprise towards stasis or constant change.

The system and its occupants will fight for the status quo, unless you prepare them for the needed changes. You must embrace the paradox that as a manager, you have to strive for repetition and predictability, a task that is impossible given the constantly changing environment in which our system resides.

Note from the Field

A division of a large multinational corporation was facing challenging external dynamics requiring potentially dramatic changes. The division had been a star performer in the glory days, considered a model of performance and predictability, but was now facing uncertain times. A young president came in bringing a new vision, new ideas, and passion. She started to make many of the needed changes. Unfortunately, she performed so well and the needs of the corporation were so great, the parent reassigned her before she had time to implement fully the necessary changes. After she left, the organization started to revert to the old comfortable behaviors and practices. The parent did not appoint a suitable replacement in time and sold the division. Despite the clear need for change as dictated by the marketplace, the organization fell back into the old comfortable patterns.

Behold: Systems can be refined to become powerful engines that reliably and repeatably make products and deliver services.

Beware: The very same management drive to lock down processes, making them repeatable and predictable, along with the desire to control the actions of your employees, can be a slippery slope to stasis.

Alfred North Whitehead said, "The art of progress is to preserve order amid change, and to preserve change amid order."[51] A grand paradox and a grand, exciting management challenge.

The remainder of this book will implore you to heed this sage advice and embrace the power of the system to be *both* predictable *and* unpredictable; *both* orderly *and* chaotic; *both* simple *and* complex; able to reside in a state of dynamic equilibrium. Beginning with Part 2 we will start to create an Enterprise Management System that is *both* repeatable, predictable, and clear, *and* at the same time fluid, poised to change in an instant.

Drucker[52] provides very clear guidance on the theory of your business. He suggests your theory will be valid if:

- ✓ The assumptions you make match reality as closely as possible. This requires deep and recurring exploration of the external and internal environments in which the enterprise resides and appropriate adjustments to purpose, vision, mission, and plans.
- ✓ The assumptions you make fit with each other. The assumptions cannot be at cross-purposes. If you have differing assumptions about the environment, you *will* have entropy in the system. You must align purpose, vision, and mission down through the organization.
- ✓ All of the occupants of the enterprise know and understand your theory. You have to ensure all the occupants understand the foundational assumptions that make up the theory. You have to ensure everyone has *shared mental models* of the enterprise and its management system.
- ✓ Your theory stands up to regular challenge. You have to challenge the basic assumptions upon which your enterprise rests and you have to revisit your Enterprise Management System regularly.

To paraphrase John Maxwell,[53] change is inevitable; progress is optional (see Chapter 14, "Change and the System," for more on change management).

Key Takeaways
- ✓ Your entire enterprise is based on a series of assumptions.
- ✓ You must review deeply and critically those assumptions.
- ✓ Go back and uncover the assumptions that underlie your thinking. Write them down in obvious terms and carefully assess their veracity.
- ✓ Beware of the grand management paradox. You have to be comfortable with the need for both ambiguity as defined by the environment and for

predictability and repeatability of the system. You must practice *both/and* thinking.

✓ You must strive to create an enterprise that is balanced dynamically, ready to change as required by the changing reality.

Recommended Reading for Chapter 3

Argyris, Chris. "Double Loop Learning in Organizations." *Harvard Business Review.* September, 1977. Argyris has written extensively, both individually and with Donald Schön, on learning and learning behaviors.

Douglas, Mary. *How Institutions Think.* Syracuse, NY: Syracuse University Press, 1986. Mary Douglas has written a must read primer for managers on how institutions take on a life of their own, driving thinking, behaviors, and performance.

Drucker, Peter F. "The Theory of the Business." *Harvard Business Review.* September–October, 1994.

Gardner, Howard. *Changing Minds.* Boston: Harvard Business School Press, 2006. Gardner's book is very helpful for managers struggling to understand their own mindsets and those of others.

Senge, Peter M. *The Fifth Discipline.* New York: Doubleday, 1990.

Part 2

The Enterprise
Management System

Chapter 4

The Most Common Management Elements

There is no new thing under the sun.
—Ecclesiastes 1:9

U p until now, we have talked about systems thinking and management of your enterprise in a generic sense. We have added an overlay of systems thinking to your existing understanding of management. However, we have thousands of years of management thought and practice to guide us in the management of the enterprise. What are we to do with all of this assembled wisdom? Do we abandon it for our new discipline of systems thinking? The answer is no. The goal of this book is to reconcile systems thinking with existing management thought. The discipline of systems thinking augments what you already know about management and vice versa. As Peter Senge proposed, systems thinking is the discipline that integrates the other disciplines. In the following chapters, we will explore how systems thinking complements the wonderful management thought that you have already absorbed.

However, one thing we do know is there is a lot of existing management thought. In fact, there may be too much. The sheer volume of management thought and the number of different management "systems" can be daunting and overwhelming. In my research, my assistants and I found over 2,400 management models.

Note from the Field

The new executive director of a not-for-profit had extensive experience in the domain of the enterprise, theater, but no experience or training in business. She had a formidable mind and a willingness to learn. She undertook to read all she could about management. Some months later at a subsequent board meeting, she was exasperated. She commented that she was now less confident in her decisions than she had been before she started reading. She said she was alternately inspired and discouraged, staggering from clarity to confusion. Finally, she said she believed the reading was just beginning to repeat itself. She asked what she should do. I suggested she stop reading and start observing the system of which she was a part. Other members of the board seconded this advice and asked me to explain systems thinking to her in more detail. At the next board meeting, she said the context provided by systems thinking brought the prior reading into focus and clarified some key tenets.

After all the years of management thought, and with the volume of methods proposed, you would think there must be a common set of functions or system elements, holons as we call them, that have emerged to help us manage the enterprise. In systems speak, we call this an *archetype*. An archetype is a pattern, construct, or set of behaviors that emerges repeatedly. As a student and professor of management and as a systems thinker, I have always been curious about such a management archetype. I thought, surely, there must be a common archetype for management. I believe there is, if you cut through the noise and confusion like our intrepid executive director. The common elements are there as an archetype in the enterprise.

Beware: Hundreds of CEOs, consultants, professors, and quacks will tell you theirs is the only method for understanding management and your enterprise, your system. Like the golfer who buys new clubs in the hope of a lower handicap or the dieter who reels from diet system to diet system in the hopes of results, simply switching to their system will not work. Your system is different from theirs. Your system is unique—unique to you, to the times, to the particular assemblage of *elements*, the particular *interactions*, the particular *purpose,* and the unique emergent properties that arise from the system and dominate the dynamics.

My explorations into such an archetype started when I first became a CEO. I was young and inexperienced and I knew I needed help and guidance. I went to a management training session put on by the Presidents Association of the American Management Association. The course was designed for owners and presidents and was primarily taught by CEOs. The content for the course was developed by asking CEOs and owners "what kept them awake at night." Over many decades the content of those answers always mapped into six key areas—leadership, culture, developing people, planning, organization, and control.[54] Another session I attended introduced me to the McKinsey Seven-S model. After consulting with thousands of companies worldwide, McKinsey derived the Seven-S Framework as a model for analyzing and managing. The Seven-S Framework incorporates strategy, structure, systems, staff, style, skills, and shared values.[55] Note the similarities between the two models.

Each of these models or frameworks was dubbed a management "system," and I became intrigued by such models. I began to research management models and, with the help of my very able research assistants,[56] discovered striking similarities. As we reviewed the over 2,400 management models and frameworks we found, we looked for commonality of management elements and terminology for evidence of an archetype.[57] We analyzed all of the models and the literature associated with them to determine the intent and scope of usage of the individual management elements embodied in each model or framework. The research resulted in a clear articulation of the most common management elements of the most common and extensively utilized management models and frameworks. They are

Governance. The enterprise system used to govern, including the board of directors.

Leadership. A formal method of assessing and developing leadership and leadership potential, both current and future, within the enterprise.

Organizational culture and climate. A formal method of understanding and assessing organizational culture, both current and future, within the enterprise.

Learning and development of employees. A formal method of assessing and developing the needed skills, capabilities, and learning, both current and potential, of all employees within the enterprise.

Strategic planning. A formal method for planning for the future of the enterprise.

Organizational structure. Clear representation of all of the organizational structure elements and dynamics embodied within the enterprise.

Control systems. All of the visible, demonstrable systems that monitor enterprise performance.

I believe the reason these elements show up repeatedly is that they are fundamental to the system. It is precisely because an enterprise is a system that the common elements emerge repeatedly. They represent an archetype of management that cannot be ignored if you are to manage effectively. These elements *will be* in evidence in your enterprise regardless of circumstances. The reason McKinsey identified them in thousands of clients and the AMA found them in the responses of thousands of CEOs is because they are *elemental* to the enterprise. The reason the models developed by dozens of top consultants and academics utilize most of the elements is because they are *fundamental* to the system.

The seven elements will be in place whether by default or design. There is a governance function at work in your enterprise whether it is active and effective or not. You will have a leadership style, effective or destructive, in your organization, by design or by default. As an emergent property of your system, you will have a corporate culture. You will have a planning process, which may be not to plan at all. These elements are inescapable and because they are *elemental* to the system, they will be *interacting* and seeking a *purpose*. Let us take each one individually.

- ✓ *Governance* has to be in evidence to set the purpose and the essential interactions through the bylaws or operating agreements.
- ✓ *Leadership* has to take the initiating purpose, drive it through the organization, approve the structure, select all the elements, and refine the interactions.
- ✓ An organizational *culture* will emerge to shape the interactions and to influence behaviors.
- ✓ There must be a method of *development* to attract, retain, and enhance the skills and competencies needed to accomplish the purpose of the system.

✓ There must be a *strategic planning* process to parse effectively the purpose and vision and to make the assignment to the elements for the system to be effective.

✓ There will be an *organizational structure* in place, and there must be clear guidance on this structure or it will emerge autopoietically.

✓ There must be *control systems* in place to provide and monitor the feedback necessary to keep the system operating.

Just like our intrepid executive director, rather than take my word or anyone else's word for the only management system that truly works, I suggest you create your own using the most common management elements. Assemble them in the way that makes sense to you. Explore the meaning of each element as it relates to *your* enterprise. Call the individual elements what you want. Stop looking for the next version of the only management system you will ever need. Acknowledge that the common elements are already at play in your enterprise. Tend to the system that is already shaping your results. Remember, your enterprise is a system perfectly designed to get the results it is getting today. All of these elements have to be present to manage the system effectively. They are *elemental*. Therefore, I believe they represent an archetype. We will use this archetype to explore further the systemic nature of management.

Figure 21 shows how I assemble the elements in my Enterprise Management System. Note: I represent the elements as holons to remind me of their systemicity and to remember to systemize each one in my enterprise.

This is the standard or default view I use. As you will see later, and because they represent a system, you can arrange the holons differently for different purposes, move

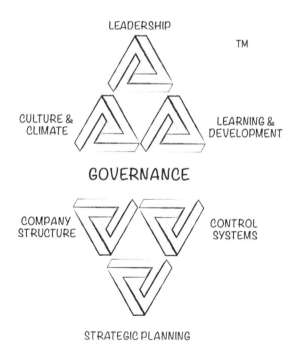

Figure 21. Archetype of the Most Common Holons

them, and aggregate them. Governance is at the center in the default view because it sets the purpose for the overall system, thereby being central. While the holons are represented individually, they never lose their systemicity. The assembled holons represent a system of systems. Remember the entreaties of Deming, Drucker, Senge, Wheatley, and others—you must assure this system is known and understood by all.[58] You must communicate the system's existence and dynamics to all. All of the occupants of the system must see and understand it hermeneutically. Your employees must know the parts and the whole. Information must flow to all, and since the holons are all connected, it will by default. You must ensure that energy and information are always flowing to, and through, all of the holons.

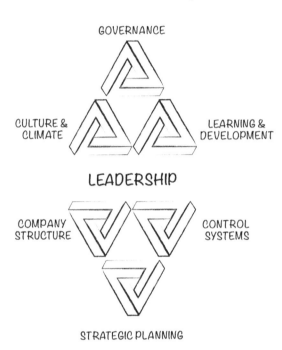

Figure 22. Urgent Centrality Shifts Central Holon

The alignment of the assembled holons retains the property of a Möbius strip; it is nonorientable. You need to become oriented to it. In this way, the holon that appears to be central can emerge as the most important element. I refer to this property as *urgent centrality*. Often the most urgent behavior or element seems to be the most important holon in the system in the short run, but is often not the most important in the long run. For instance, once governance is set, it often recedes to the background and leadership becomes the central holon as shown in Figure 22.

Urgent centrality can be a powerful emergent property of systems. Used as a diagnostic tool, it can bring to light key dynamics of the system and cause management to focus on that element. For instance, when the way forward becomes unclear, the need for strategic planning often becomes central to the enterprise and begins to become a central driving dynamic until the planning process is completed or the current plan reviewed.

Beware: The holons never lose their systemicity and are constantly connected to and communicating with the larger system. As this example from a family business describes, urgent centrality can mask more important system dynamics.

Note from the Field

The patriarch of a successful enterprise was in declining health, and members from his extended family and his advisors were concerned about the state of the business. Their focus was on the leadership void his declining health and lack of succession planning were creating. The enterprise was expending an extraordinary amount of physical and emotional energy trying, unsuccessfully, to resolve the leadership issue between the father and his children who were unqualified to run the business. This focus on leadership was admirable and urgent, but far more important was the question of governance. There was no effective governance structure in place to reconcile system challenges in his absence and so all of the confusion around leadership and succession would merely devolve into legal and estate-driven actions that could significantly disrupt effective system dynamics. Hence, governance, not leadership was the most important system holon to be managed at that time.

Recursive Pattern Redux

You will remember from the system-thinking tenets that systems often repeat in recursive patterns. Thus, it is with the most common holons. The common holons archetype repeats itself throughout the enterprise. Governance sets the purpose for the system at the next level down in the organization, and leadership takes over from there. All of the other common holons are then present in a departmental management system as shown in Figure 23. Note: there *will* be different elements, interactions, and purpose for each of the subordinate systems, which you must align with the overall system and purpose. This is normal. In the following chapters dedicated to each holon, we will explore how to accomplish this specialization, while retaining system integrity.

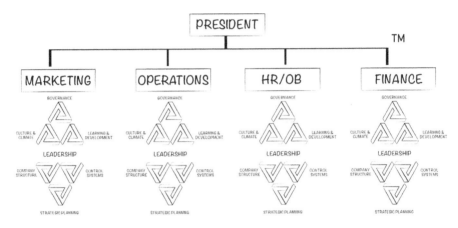

Figure 23. Recursive Archetype

Reassembly

Since holons are both parts of the system and inseparable from the whole system, you can merge them into greater wholes. Often consultants talk about "soft" systems and "hard" systems. They make this distinction because the soft systems are difficult to measure and therefore soft, whereas the hard systems can have clear descriptions and are easy to measure. Organizational charts, strategic plans, and control means all have concrete, often iconic, representations, whereas leadership, culture, climate, and development are harder to assess.

> **Beware:** Wheatley and others specifically caution managers against relying on the more easily quantified hard systems as a more correct or specific way in which to manage. Just because an element or holon is easier to measure and track does not mean it is a good measure of system health or efficacy or a better part of the system. The *soft* elements are more subtle and cannot be addressed as directly, yet they are powerful determinants of system performance.

Wheatley states this caution perfectly:

We tried for many years to avoid the messiness and complexity of being human, and now that denial is coming back to haunt us. We keep failing to create outcomes and changes we need in organizations because we continue to deny that "the human element" is anything but a "soft" and not to be taken seriously minor distraction.[59]

Figure 24 shows a view of the system broken into hard and soft holons.

How finely you parse your enterprise system depends on your purpose; remember, however, whatever element or holon you are looking at never loses its systemicity.

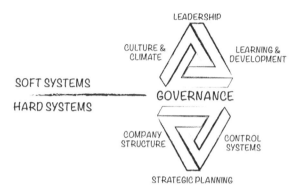

Figure 24. Reassembled Holons as Hard and Soft

Key Takeaways

✓ The most common holons of *governance, leadership, culture and climate, learning and development, strategic planning, organizational structure,* and *control systems* (the archetype) are at play in your enterprise, either by design or by default.

✓ You can use the holons as diagnostic tools; a set of lenses you can use to look for systemic problems in your enterprise.

✓ Systems often present an urgent dynamic that may, or may not, be the most important dynamic at that time. A holistic, systems view can often reveal the more important holon.

✓ The system is not static. You must constantly evaluate and update the holons of your enterprise management model to ensure your model is appropriate for the time and circumstances.

Recommended Reading for Chapter 4

Collins, James C. *Good to Great: Why Some Companies Make the Leap and Others Don't.* New York: Harper Collins, 2001. While not overtly systems-thinking books, both of Collins's books recommended here offer a wealth of information on creating a powerful management system.

Collins, James C., and Jerry I. Porras. *Built to Last: Successful Habits of Visionary Companies.* New York: Harper Business, 1994.

Deming, W. Edwards. *The New Economics for Industry, Government, and Education.* Cambridge: MIT Press, 1993.

Meadows, Donella H. *Thinking in Systems*. White River Junction: Chelsea Green Publishing Company, 2008.

Senge, Peter M. *The Fifth Discipline*. New York: Doubleday, 1990.

Wheatley, Margaret J. *Leadership and the New Science: Discovering Order in a Chaotic World*. San Francisco: Berrett-Koehler Publishers, 2006.

Chapter 5

The System at Work

In order to properly understand the big picture, everyone should fear becoming mentally clouded and obsessed with one small section of truth.
—Xun Zi[60]

Xun Zi's wise words should resonate with you now that you have a systems perspective. In most enterprises, people focus on "one small section of truth." While this focus can be important and rewarding, you must remember *both/and* thinking. Everyone in the system must be aware of *both* their part in the system *and* the whole system. This chapter looks at ways to view the system in its most complete terms as a series of simple mental models.

Beware: The models presented here are simplified representations of the real system. We know simplicity is an artifice to help us understand the more complex and nuanced whole. Models are both simple and complex. They should encourage us to look beyond the simplicity to the more nuanced reality.

Remember that in Chapter 2 we discussed how Wheatley and others proposed a view of the system and its values, vision, and occupants as a series of fields. I derive the first model for enterprise effectiveness from this concept and from the law of conservation of energy. You and your employees are expending energy every day. Is it directed properly?

Enterprise Model #1: Energy Flow in the Organization

We know from the law of conservation of energy that energy is neither created nor destroyed. You must account for all of it. Theoretically, if we had a perfect conductor there would be no loss of energy. In systems speak the throughput would be perfect and energy in would equal energy out.

$$E_{IN} = E_{OUT}$$

However, we know that perfect conductors do not exist. Therefore, the equation looks like this:

$$E_{IN} = E_{OUT} - \underline{LOSSES}$$

In our case, losses take on the form of entropy and Brownian motion, the random forces or counterproductive actions that derive from system inconsistencies in our enterprise system. If we can minimize these destructive dynamics, we can optimize throughput as shown in Figure 25.

MANAGEMENT'S JOB IS TO MINIMIZE
SYSTEM LOSSES TO MAXIMIZE THROUGHPUT

Figure 25. Enterprise Model #1

Throughput then becomes a function of our Enterprise Management System. As Deming, Goldratt, and others have cautioned, we must be constantly aware of the system effects on performance and of the bottlenecks that exist within the processes and systems we have created. We see clearly that our system is perfectly designed to get the results it is getting. To improve results, we must improve total system throughput. To improve throughput, we must improve the *total* system, *not* any one part or person. To do this we must take a holistic approach. We must holistically evaluate the whole and the parts and, perhaps, traverse through the hermeneutic circle several times to see clearly the whole story.

Enterprise Model #2: Business Cycle

Next, let us look at how our system of systems plays out in our business cycle. Described years ago, and shown in Figure 26, the basic business cycle begins with a plan inserted into the company (the system), which is made up of people (employees), who act according to the plan, and results emerge—the transformation of inputs into outputs.

This basic business model is a simple, high-level mental model of any business. From this simple construct, we can derive a powerful diagnostic equation for results, for system throughput (see Figure 27).

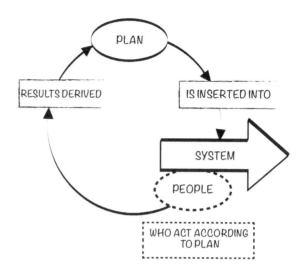

Figure 26. Basic Business Cycle

You will note the function is a product. If any element rates low on the scale, it drags down the whole. In other words, it is a *bottleneck* and it *constrains* system throughput. Optimizing any one of the elements individually does not significantly improve system throughput unless it is at the bottleneck. Counterintuitively, you

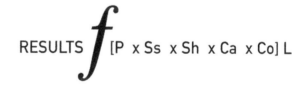

$$\text{RESULTS} \int [P \times Ss \times Sh \times Ca \times Co] L$$

P = QUALITY OF PLAN
Ss = QUALITY OF SOFT SYTEMS
Sh = QUALITY OF HARD SYSTEMS
Ca = CAPABILITIES OF PEOPLE
Co = COMMITMENT OF PEOPLE

Figure 27. Enterprise Model #2

may have to suboptimize one part of the system to optimize system throughput. For example, you could have the very best plan in the industry to capture a twenty million dollar opportunity with a customer, and have great people capable of executing the plan, but if your organization and processes are not capable of that throughput, the plan is not going to work. So you have to scale the plan back (suboptimize the plan) in order to accomplish the most with the system.

Beware: Remember bottlenecks migrate. If you remove the bottleneck in one area of the system, it will migrate to another part of the system. In this example, if you fix the plan, but you do not train the people in the new systems, they will be overwhelmed and become the bottleneck.

Let us look at all of the variables in the equation individually.

- *Quality of the plan.* This variable ties directly back to one of the most common holons in the most common management systems—strategic planning. If you do not have an effective way to develop a strategic plan that rigorously evaluates the external and internal environments and signals the key changes you must make to assure your enterprise stays aligned with the shifts in the marketplace, results are bound to be compromised. Similarly, if you do not have an effective planning methodology that includes employees and key contributors and invests them in the need for change, resistance is inevitable. Read more on these dynamics in Chapter 10, "Planning in the System." (Also, refer to the works of Porter, Prahalad, Bartlett and Ghoshal, and others listed in the suggested readings section at the end of each chapter.)
- *Quality of the soft systems.* This variable relates to the efficacy of your soft system holons. How effective and appropriate is your leadership style and that of your managers? Is your culture, a powerful emergent property of the system, beneficial or detrimental to system performance? Are the occupants of your system developing as required by the plan? Do they know both their role and how it is changing? Do they know the system, and how it is changing? Read more on these dynamics in Chapters 7, 8, and 9. (Also, refer to the works of Drucker, Kotter, Bennis, and others listed in the suggested readings section at the end of each chapter.)
- *Quality of the hard systems.* This variable relates directly to the quality of your processes and management subsystems. Are your processes well-constructed and reviewed for efficacy? Is your organizational structure clear, and does it align with the plan? Are roles and responsibilities clearly articulated? Are your processes, feedback, and control systems properly aligned? Read more on these dynamics in Chapters 11 and 12. (Also, refer to the works of Deming, Goldratt, Hammer, Champy, and others listed in the suggested readings section at the end of each chapter).
- *Capabilities and commitment of the people.* These variables focus on whether you have, in the words of Jim Collins, "the right people on the bus."[61] Do the people have the right skills and attitudes for the roles they are expected

to play? Do they have the right tools, training, and aptitude individually? Do they understand the system they are working in? Read more on these dynamics in Chapters 7, 8, and 9. (Also, refer to the works of Collins, Charan, Senge, Welch, and others listed in the suggested readings section at the end of each chapter.)

- *Luck.* The final variable is luck. Alas, the best managers are always subject to the vagaries and vicissitudes of the marketplace. I hope that systems thinking and a properly constructed Enterprise Management System will allow you to benefit from luck more often than not. Remember Louis Pasteur's entreaty that "fortune favors the prepared mind."[62] Similarly, numerous sources including Thomas Jefferson have been reported to proclaim, "I am a great believer in luck, and I find the harder I work, the more I have of it."

Enterprise Model #3: Sum of the Efforts

The final, simple equation to spur your management thought is shown in Figure 28.

We must always remember the enterprise is an assemblage of the people in it, hence the importance of the *soft* system holons. Many organizations state as a value that their people are their most important asset. Yet, if you do not optimize the system they are in, you will actually send mixed, counterproductive, and often hurtful messages unintentionally.

$$RESULTS = \sum_{N=1}^{\infty} INDIVIDUAL\ EFFORTS$$

Figure 28. Enterprise Model #3

Beware: Margaret Wheatley's images of organizations as soulless, sterile constructs[63] and Gareth Morgan's image of the organization as a "psychic prison"[64] should be chilling reminders of the power of the system to enslave the occupants.

As Drucker, Deming, Senge, and others have implored, it is the primary responsibility of leaders, individually but mostly as a team, to identify, analyze, and improve systemic weaknesses (poorly designed subsystems), and to maximize system throughput and condition. Senge's entreaty to build a learning organization, filled with learning individuals, who are enmeshed in a learning management system should be the clarion call.

We are right back to *both/and* thinking. These models and equations reiterate the basic system-thinking tenets and the importance of *both/and* thinking. Results, performance, throughput, whatever term we want to use, are a function of *both* the system *and* the individual, *both* the system *and* the team, *both* the system *and* the subsystems. The system is pervasive, but the people run the system, and you design the system and manage the people in it.

The Common Holons and the System

Bringing together the most common holons, the archetypal system, as found in the management literature and the concept of the enterprise as a force field with amplitude, direction, and subsystems, we can now construct a complete view of the Enterprise Management System.

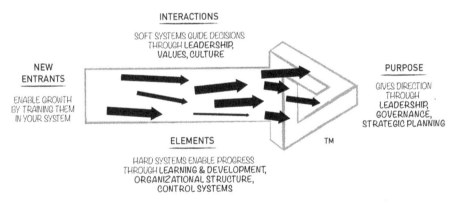

Figure 29. Enterprise Management System (EMS)

In Figure 29, we see the three components of a system—*purpose, elements, and interactions*. These are further refined as soft elements and hard elements of our system, and given further clarity by the most common holons, which are elemental to the system.

- Governance, leadership, and planning all serve to shape the purpose of the system.
- Leadership, culture, and values, the foundation of culture, serve to shape the interactions and guide our decisions and shape the commitment of our people

- Learning, development, structure, and control systems serve to enable progress and growth and help build the capabilities of our people.

Finally, our system is an open system that can accept new entrants who support our growth.

In the following chapters, we will explore each of the most common holons in depth, and consider how systems thinking influences each one.

Key Takeaways

✓ The enterprise can be described using three basic, simple equations that illuminate the power of the system tenets.

✓ You must focus on total system throughput when you evaluate individuals, processes, elements, subsystems, etc.

✓ Throughput is a function of both the individuals and the system.

✓ Point or local optimization can be counterproductive and often harmful.

✓ Counterintuitively, it is often necessary to suboptimize certain subsystems to optimize total system throughput.

✓ The system becomes a powerful, enveloping construct. You must view and manage it holistically.

Recommended Reading for Chapter 5

Deming, W. Edwards. *The New Economics for Industry, Government, and Education.* Cambridge: MIT Press, 1993.

Drucker, Peter F. *The Essential Drucker.* New York: Harper, 2001.

Goldratt, Eliyahu M. *The Goal: A Process of Ongoing Improvement.* Great Barrington: North River Press, 1984.

Senge, Peter M. *The Fifth Discipline.* New York: Doubleday, 1990.

Wheatley, Margaret J. *Leadership and the New Science: Discovering Order in a Chaotic World.* San Francisco: Berrett-Koehler Publishers, 2006.

Chapter 6

Governance in the System

He who has the gold, rules.
—Various

Most management books start with leadership because they are written for leaders and leadership is the critical, often defining, holon once the system is set on its course, once the purpose has been established. However, governance is the holon that sets the purpose for the whole system, by default or by design. Therefore, it is critical to understand the pervasive and powerful nature of governance. The governance function is often the most opaque and mysterious element of the Enterprise Management System. It often remains hidden for long periods, or is subsumed in other system elements.

For instance, in small and family businesses, governance is often an extension of the owner or the family unit. The founder is CEO and performs the function of governance. Similarly, in many not-for-profits, the board is an active participant in the other system elements, often intimately involved in leadership roles. In government organizations, the governance holon can be subject to, and responsible for, political, philosophical, and ideological dynamics that may have a dramatic impact on the enterprise.

In the above instances, governance and its impact can dwell unexamined for long periods, emerging only in times of crisis. Times of crisis are not often good times to experience the power of the holon of governance. As the Note from the Field in Chapter 3 about the family patriarch in declining health revealed, governance remained hidden from the other members of the system. Since he alone had knowledge of this function, the other members of the system remained focused on leadership and operational issues, unaware of, and unprepared for, the potentially catastrophic change his absence would bring to their reality and environment.

You must learn to orient yourself to the governance holon, to observe its effects while maintaining an understanding of its connectedness, its "systemicity." In all of the above scenarios, the practice of holistic thinking and the mental models of holons can be powerful management tools for you to understand where and how governance issues may be affecting system performance. Note: If you are manager and have no say in or access to governance, you might be tempted to ignore it. That is a mistake. Even if you have no ability to influence the governance function, the function will influence the environment in which you operate—silently shaping your reality. Therefore, you must at least consider the impact governance is having on your reality.

Soft and Hard Systems

In Figure 30, you will note that governance exhibits both soft and hard characteristics. The bylaws, corporate documents, and legal structure provide clear, "hard," guidance to the enterprise. However, governance also exhibits soft system dynamics that can dramatically shape enterprise action. Governance sets a philosophy for the enterprise that can be superior to other system dynamics. In the hierarchy of business dynamics, the philosophy promulgated by the governance function, and manifest in defining policies, takes precedence over other dynamics, often invisibly.

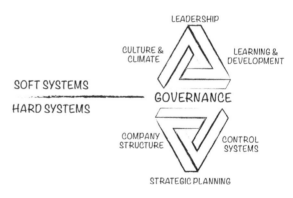

Figure 30. Governance as Soft and Hard Holons

Governance as Philosophy

Governance sets the context for the enterprise by establishing the purpose and setting beliefs and policies, what I call *contextual engineering*. Max De Pree wrote, "Beliefs come before policies or standards or practice."[65] These beliefs often remain invisible or unchallenged like the assumptions that underlie our theory of the business. Yet, James Harvey Robinson, the great American historian, cautioned,

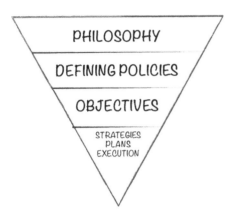

Figure 31. Business Hierarchy

"We are incredibly heedless in the formation of our beliefs, but find ourselves filled with an illicit passion for them when anyone proposes to rob us of their companionship."[66] Figure 31 reflects the hierarchical nature of how the philosophy formed in the governance function holds sway over the enterprise.

Similar to the way culture emerges out of the system, the enterprise beliefs, the philosophy, can creep into existence and remain hidden from view. We will often defend the philosophy as "the way we have always done it" without questioning its veracity and appropriateness. Stemming from governance, these philosophical emanations can appear to be off-limits to management. It is important to explore the governance holon for such hidden impacts. These often hidden beliefs must be explicit and clear, for their existence will be revealed by the system and the actions of the leaders in the system.

Beware: Typically, philosophy is manifest in values statements, but often critical and powerful values from governance are unwritten. Although unstated, these values very prominently act on the enterprise.

Note from the Field

The majority owner of a company had very successfully started and grown a government contracting services firm. He was adamantly wedded to providing only services to the federal government. He did not want to invest in commercial or product activities. This aversion became a part of the philosophy of the enterprise and promulgated through successive boards and management leaders as defining policy even after the owner disengaged from the business. Although these strictures were unwritten, and increasingly counterproductive, the organization never formally challenged their existence or veracity. As the restrictive philosophy became increasingly counterproductive, senior management began to explore changes that would challenge the unwritten rules. I repeatedly inquired of senior management where the board (governance) stood on the proposed changes and was assured that the board was inactive, benign and, most importantly, supportive of current management. It turns out nothing could have been further from the truth. Repeatedly, the owner, supported by an out-of-touch board, rebuffed important strategic initiatives because they violated the unwritten rules of the philosophy. Consequently, the company missed the industry shift to commercial markets and product-based solutions, resulting in the loss of a leading position and a dramatic erosion of value.

Your board members and you must be conscious of the power governance has to influence system performance and response through action, inaction, and comments. As prior notes have revealed, you should remember that occupants of the system will formulate assumptions from your actions and words that may not reflect what you intended. Quine and Ullian in their illuminating treatise on belief, *The Web of Belief*, summarized the hidden characteristic of belief: "Believing is a disposition that can linger latent and unobserved. It is a disposition to respond in certain ways when the appropriate issue arises."[67] In *The Way Institutions Think*, Mary Douglas also underscores the power of hidden belief and philosophy to shape thought: "An answer is only seen to be the right one if it sustains the institutional thinking that is already in the minds of individuals as they try to decide."[68]

Family businesses and sole proprietorships should take heed of the importance and power of governance. Family businesses often equate governance with family dynamics and vice versa.

Note from the Field

I worked with a family business that was struggling with a number of business issues that all revolved around succession planning and generational transition. The business itself was in a good industry and capable of performing well. A husband and wife owned the business. Their sons, as well as some daughters-in-law, all worked in the business. When I inquired as to the governance function and whether the enterprise had a board, the family proudly announced that they did have a board. Upon further inquiry, the structure of the board was revealed— the father, mother, and sons. Hence, governance and leadership, two of the most critical systems holons, were blurred and compromised. Without the benefit of outside input, the family struggled to make good decisions about the business. Family dynamics overwhelmed good business decisions eventually driving a wedge between family members.

In this case, a separate governance function, with some outside opinions, could have easily resolved the business issues and potentially removed the family issues from the business. A family business constitution outlining the purpose, goals, and practices of the business and delineating family, business, and governance roles could have resolved most of the issues and preserved a valuable asset. See Chapter 16, "Family Businesses and the System," for more information on family constitutions.

Not-for-profit enterprises often struggle with governance. There are several reasons for this. Powerful members will often flex the organization and its purpose to their will by force of personality, financial support, or both. Management may not be able to do much about this dynamic. However, realizing that this is your reality and designing the system in response can minimize frustration. Executive directors often rely on board members for day-to-day tasks, but cannot hold them accountable or feel that they cannot give them strong guidance or feedback. Training board members in systems thinking and your Enterprise Management System can be powerful steps, leading to better understanding of roles.

Finally, a note about government entities in regards to governance. Government agencies are often unintentionally set at cross-*purposes* by legislation or changes in leadership. In these cases, it is important to identify the specific system dynamic that may be driving the friction.

Note from the Field

I worked with two government agencies charged with similar, complementary missions. I was engaged to do team building assessments and exercises at the request of both department heads, due to excessive friction. The two departments were constantly battling and customer service scores were very poor. Using systems thinking, we were quickly able to show each side that their purposes and processes needed to be aligned very closely and that the resulting customer deliverable was dependent on close cooperation. They were codependent, and each team began to realize they were practicing bounded rationality, compromising system throughput and quality. In fact, the employees from each department wanted to work closely with and respect the other. We were able to determine that the friction was primarily a result of poor statutory language and oversight by the state authority that had set the purpose for each department. By clarifying the source of the system problems, the department heads were able to approach their bosses and reconcile the issues at the appropriate level. Even as this unbalanced force remained unsolved, the departments began to work more closely together on their own. The directors met at their level and aligned the two departments' purposes. The staffs no longer clashed, because they realized their counterparts were aligned with them. The conflict remained at the directors' level until the legislature resolved the issue, leaving the staffs, and their systems, to optimize throughput at their level.

Governance is so powerful that it can seem immovable. Legal or regulatory constraints are real after all. However, often issues that seem immovable are artifacts of long-standing assumptions that over time have come to be perceived as bedrock. It is incumbent on you to deeply explore the governance holon in your enterprise for hidden power. Board members must be trained in the power of governance to drive system behaviors. Finally, family members must practice the discipline of stepping out of their normal roles and into their governance roles with clarity and transparency.

Here are some things you can do, and questions you should ask, to explore and improve the governance holon in your system:

1. Acknowledge the existence of governance as a powerful system component, already at work in your enterprise.
2. Review the holon systemically. Is the purpose of governance in your enterprise clearly understood and articulated? What are the elements that make up the holon? Are they the correct elements for effective system performance? Are the interactions of the holon itself, and with the other holons of the system, appropriate, beneficial, and clear?
3. Ask yourself, "Does my governance holon provide a clear, compelling, purpose to the leadership of the enterprise?" If you alone represent the governance function in your enterprise, ask yourself, "Am I clear and honest with the purpose I have established for my enterprise? Have I articulated that purpose?"
4. Consider establishing your own "board," even if you are a sole proprietor. This can be a mentor, a board of advisors, or a formal board. Leading an enterprise can be a lonely, confusing job. Having trusted advisors who will help you, challenge you, and refine your thinking can be very powerful.
5. If you have a board, establish a formal board orientation that includes systems-thinking training. Discussing this holon with your board can often illuminate unstated dynamics and open a dialogue.

Key Takeaways

✓ Governance is often silent or ignored until its supremacy takes charge in moments of crisis. Crisis is usually not an ideal time to deal with this holon. You must be aware of the governance holon at all times and orient yourself to it.

✓ Individuals serving in both governance and leadership roles in the system must be aware of the different viewpoints of the system derived from the different roles.

✓ While governance recedes into the background during most enterprise life spans, it remains the most powerful holon, capable of dramatically changing enterprise direction and dynamics. Both board members and management must be aware of how powerful, and often silent, this enterprise system dynamic is.

✓ Beliefs and philosophies from governance often silently and powerfully hold sway over enterprises. You must be aware of these dynamics.

✓ You may have to "manage up" to reconcile governance issues that manifest themselves at your level in the system.

Recommended Reading for Chapter 6

Deming, W. Edwards. *The New Economics for Industry, Government, and Education.* Cambridge: MIT Press, 1993.

Drucker, Peter F. *The Essential Drucker.* New York: Harper, 2001.

Gardner, Howard. *Changing Mindsets.* Boston: Harvard Business School Press, 2006.

Nadler, David A., Beverly A. Behan, and Mark B. Nadler. *Building Better Boards.* San Francisco: Jossey-Bass, 2006. If you are serious about good governance and having a high-performing board, this book is a must read.

Sinek, Simon. *Start with Why.* New York: Penguin, 2009. Sinek has written a great book on clarifying purpose and answering the question why. Governance is at the heart of this question.

Chapter 7

Leadership in the System

Uneasy lies the head that wears a crown.
—Shakespeare[69]

*Leadership is an art, something to be learned over time, not
simply by reading books. Leadership is more tribal than scientific,
more a weaving of relationships than an amassing of information.*
—Max De Pree[70]

L eadership in all its manifestations—position, process, potential—becomes the most powerful and central holon in the system *after* the initial purpose of the system is set by governance. Leadership alone has the vision and authority to design and develop the Enterprise Management System or the dangerous luxury to ignore that work and let the system develop by default.

- Leadership picks the elements of the system.
- Leadership receives the purpose from governance and has the responsibility to assure assimilation and alignment of purpose throughout the enterprise.
- Leadership sets the tone for the systemic interactions.

Authors and scholars have written extensively about leadership and offered much management guidance. However, much of it is has been offered without the context afforded by systems thinking. Now that you have a foundation in systems thinking, you should perceive the need for a change in the leader's role. In the system, leadership is not just about decisions, actions, and direction: a leader must cultivate two critical traits, systems thinking and humility. In addition to all the other leadership traits espoused by other authors, you need to cultivate these two traits to unlock the power of the system you set in motion, a system that takes on a life of its own. Leading in the system requires subtle shifts in leadership type and style, and the higher you rise in the enterprise, the more pronounced the shift. The important shifts are as follows:

1. You must shift from leading only with action and direction, to leading through guidance after sensing the dynamics of the system.
2. You must shift to using *both/and* thinking, engaging both the left and right sides of the brain—being both systemic and systematic.
3. You must shift from looking only down into your organization to looking at your impact upon it.
4. You must shift from viewing the enterprise only as a hierarchy designed for control, to viewing it in systems terms, as a holarchy assembled from the bottom up.
5. You must shift from a relentless focus on the numbers and the hard systems, to an equal embrace of the soft systems holons.

Let me explain each shift and the influence on leadership in the system.

Lead through Guidance

The first leadership shift is a shift from leading through action to leading through guidance. Daniel Goleman,[71] through his seminal book *Emotional Intelligence*, has been instrumental in introducing the importance of emotional intelligence to effective leadership. In my experience consulting with enterprises of all types, most managers admit to reacting to situations too quickly and immediately trying to solve a problem. Before getting themselves oriented to the system and looking for second-order dynamics and assumptions, they start acting. The first shift in leadership thinking in a systems environment is a shift from action leadership to thought and emotional leadership.

Looking again at the business hierarchy, you must be sensitive to the systemic, philosophic, and policy implications of your decisions. Remembering how the basic holons are replicated down through the organization, you now represent the governance function *within* your system holon (see Figure 32). You must think beyond the simple, single loop solution to the problem and look for the systems implications. Implications, often removed in time and space by delays, oftentimes considerably. The implications may be a migration of the local bottleneck to a more precarious bottleneck elsewhere in the system or a significant point optimization locally that compromises another system element or interaction far removed.

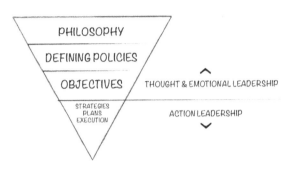

Figure 32. Shift in Leadership

As a leader, you should be the first and most likely node in the system to sense system problems. Problems such as an invisible philosophy that compromises system performance, or departments that are at cross-purposes, or personnel who are practicing bounded rationality. Remember Deming's finding that 94 percent of the defects, errors, mistakes, and misunderstandings are systemic. You have to sense these sorts of systemic challenges first and guide the other elements of the system to reconcile them.

This does not mean that action leadership is not important, even critical. Action leadership is doing things. It is dynamic, proactive, and anticipatory. We all rose to positions of leadership in our current and prior organizations by exhibiting action leadership. Action leadership is a *loud* skill and you will still have to use it regularly. However, real understanding and success at the higher levels of the holarchy require the addition of different leadership dynamics—thought and emotional leadership. Thought and emotional leadership are very different from action leadership. They require different skills—skills such as listening, probing, reflecting, guiding, and mentoring. Thought and emotional leadership are *quiet* skills. They are required to sense and elicit the beliefs and philosophic basis for policies and practices.

> **Behold:** The same powerful system dynamic that has the elements of the system constantly communicating provides you with a constant stream of signals about system health, *if* you will listen, observe, and sense. First, you must stop acting and start observing.

I have been conducting an informal survey of managers and students for over twenty-five years on the prevalence of training in listening and observation skills and techniques. Less than 5 percent of the respondents—directors, students, managers, CEOs, leaders of all types—have studied or been trained in listening and observing skills! Various researchers report that on average we hear properly only 25–50 percent of what is said to us. There are many reasons for this including lack of interest, ambient activity, philosophical differences, and more urgent concerns. The small percentage we do properly hear is generally enough to give us the gist of what is said, but what about the essence? What about the subtle, nonverbal cues?

As a rule, we are not good at listening and sensing skills. Most of us listen and observe with our response track playing in the background and our prevailing mental model filtering our view, ready and eager to deliver *our* message or opinion. Using this form of observation, we are almost completely tone deaf to our audience. Leadership authors recommend *active listening* (or appreciative listening). Active listening is listening with more than just your ears. It involves engaging the person and using your eyes and heart to search for meaning, nuance, and understanding. It is critical to sensing the *totality* of the information conveyed. Active listening includes

- empathizing with the speaker.
- avoiding interruptions.
- making eye contact.
- maintaining interest.
- postponing evaluation.
- paraphrasing information.
- sending signals back to the speaker that they are important and their message is heard.

Dr. Albert Mehrabian of UCLA famously highlighted how much information is conveyed in the two nonverbal elements of speech—tone of voice and body language. In many situations, tone of voice and body language dominate the transmission of information, swamping the words.[72] Leadership needs to be aware of how powerful tone of voice and body language are and how they can transmit messages to the system regardless of words.

Note from the Field

I worked with a family business that strove to minimize the impact on the business of a deep family rift by conscientiously avoiding talking about family issues in the workplace. They specifically set aside times and places outside of the company facilities to conduct these, often contentious, discussions. Unfortunately, their subsequent tone and body language in the facilities and among employees clearly demonstrated the animosity between the factions. Under these conditions, employees became even more concerned, and since they had no information about what was really going on, they made up the story that completed the hermeneutic circle in their minds. The employees private mental narratives, ranging from the selling of the business to shutting it down, were often far worse than the potential real or contemplated outcomes. The system is always communicating and sending information and signals. In the absence of real information, the occupants will complete the hermeneutic circle and derive their own story.

Beware: As many of our modern communications become electronic, you must realize that the *recipient* of your emails, texts, and tweets will *imply* tone of voice and body language. You are not in control of this reception; the recipient is. The words are not delivered with any attached tone, so it is up to the recipient to imply the tone. A message you send to your controller that says, "What is going on?" could be received as "Sales are soaring—tell me about the good news," or "With these soaring sales, cash flow is anemic—what are you doing about it?" Both of these dynamics could be occurring at the same time, and it is the controller who decides which one you are referring to by the tone he assumes is implied in the message.

Once you have sensed, observed, and explored the systemic implications, action is called for. We are back to Boyd's OODA loop caution: make sure you *orient* yourself before you act. Acting while disoriented can lead to disaster. The need to use thought and emotional leadership becomes more pronounced the higher one ascends in the enterprise. System-of-systems interactions and dynamics are often hidden or delayed, and these filters become more prevalent as one rises in the hierarchy. Accordingly, a manager's approach to leadership must change. Figure 33 reflects the growing importance of this shift in leadership style.

The scale is not meant to be precise or prescriptive. It is there to highlight the importance of the shift in leadership from action leadership to observation and guidance.

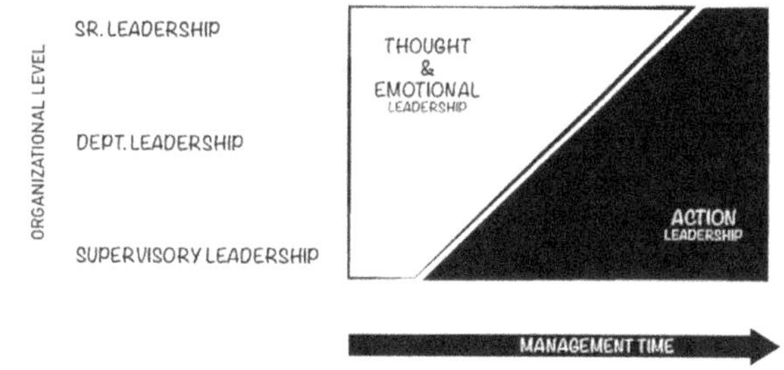

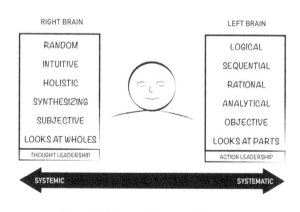

Figure 33. Shift in Leadership Style

Both Systemic and Systematic

The second leadership shift is a shift to *both/and* thinking—to thinking systemically and systematically. There is a subtle but profound difference between those two words and concepts. Thinking *systematically* relates to action leadership and implies we are taking action to systematize some portion of our function. Thinking *systemically* relates to thought and emotional leadership and implies we are stepping back from the system and viewing it holistically.

Adding thought and emotional leadership to your repertoire of skills may be difficult for some. Most of us rose to positions of influence and leadership in our organizations by practicing action leadership. We are good at it. Action leadership usually involves engaging the left side of the brain, the logical, sequential, analytical side. This type of leadership is critical to execution and

Figure 34. Systemic versus Systematic

driving results. You do not need to abandon it. There will continue to be times you will need it, often extensively. It represents the *systematic* approach so critical to making our enterprises predictable and repeatable.

However, you must balance this with the *systemic* thinking of the right side of the brain. This side of the brain takes the holistic view and deals with randomness, ambiguity, and creativity. It is intuitive and synthesizing, making sense out of randomness and connecting dots. Figure 34 compares the thinking traits of the brain's left and right sides.

All humans have and use both sides of their brain: however, one side is usually more developed and dominates the way we process the information we get from all our senses. Left-brain linear thinkers often do not see the connections between system elements clearly. Importantly, since they are not associative thinkers, they struggle to see the importance of random bits of data. They have trouble "connecting the dots" as easily as right-brain thinkers do. Often they cannot make sense of nonlogical, ambiguous environments. This leads them to deduce that the information is too hard to understand, is not connected, is not important, or all of the foregoing. This blindness makes dealing with ambiguity and uncertainty difficult. It is very uncomfortable and disorienting.

Interestingly, Charles Sanders Peirce, in his penetrating treatise *The Fixation of Beliefs*,[73] suggests this state of disorientation and discomfort is the *only* state in which we are open to changing *our* beliefs, our internal mental models or schema about the reality in which we are enmeshed. The most common response to this disorientation is to retreat to our old comfortable models and beliefs to regain a feeling of being in control. This is very dangerous for you as a leader, charged with making sense of just such environments. The practice of thought and emotional leadership in times like these is critical. As a leader, you have to resist the urge to act, until you are oriented, until you have checked your beliefs and mental models for veracity. Unfortunately, as you have no doubt experienced, some sort of crisis that begs for action usually accompanies these ambiguous and disquieting periods. This is yet another management paradox for you to contemplate!

Always using a systematic approach, also explains why so many organizations and managers struggle with effective strategic planning and change management: the first step, according to Boyd's OODA loop, is to observe, or to seek to analyze and understand the environment, which is highly random and ambiguous. The tendency to revert to our comfortable mental models makes it hard to make new connections and see relative importance. Not surprisingly, left-brain dominant, systematic managers tend to focus on the internal workings and processes of the company or their department. Often these same managers originally constructed this world, and to them it is linear, logical, sequential, and therefore, safe and understandable.

> **Beware:** A left-brain dominant systematic mindset in a manger often leads them to view the system as a collection of parts they can optimize (point optimization) using action leadership techniques. Since they have not made the connections in the system, they do not see the systemic importance and connections. They are disoriented. Their arrow may even be pointing in the wrong direction.

Conversely, right-brain thinkers can more easily see the connections and make the associations in the marketplace and the system, but they may have a difficult time prioritizing and converting that into logical, linear, sequential action plans.

Again, people often exhibit a strength or preference for one side of the brain or the other. However, you should use the two styles in tandem. You must work to utilize both sides of the brain and to balance the impulses and importance of each. Similarly, you need to embrace the different styles on your teams, and use the diversity of viewpoints and opinions to explore fully system issues.

Two skills are critical: the self-awareness to understand your preferences, and the ability to discern when to use left-brain action leadership and when to pause and use right-brain emotional and thought leadership. In design thinking, IDEO, the legendary design and innovation firm, refers to these different phases as "flare" and "focus."[74] There are times when you and your team need to flare, sense the system and explore alternate schema, approaches, and mental models, and times when you need to focus and execute.

Understanding Your Impact on the System

> *You must be the change you wish to see in the world.*
> —Gandhi

The third leadership shift begins with assessing your impact on the system. As managers, we spend a lot of time looking down into the organization and at individual parts, elements, or people. This shift involves looking at the impact of your leadership style, mental models, and preferences on the system. It is not an easy task, and being honest about the effect of your leadership on the organization can be hard.

Note from the Field

One of companies I led had been a start-up. I was one of the first employees in the company. As CEO, I managed the creation of every function and department and hired all the department heads. I used many of the techniques I espouse here, and we were highly successful—headed for an IPO. I thought I had created a wonderful work environment and a great Enterprise Management System. Following standard practice, we surveyed our employees for their assessment of leadership. I expected to receive good results, and I was looking forward to using the findings to make the enterprise even better. However, the results of the survey stung. Overall, our employees reported being engaged, motivated, and very satisfied with management. However, my direct reports had a different story to tell. While they liked and respected me, they indicated my leadership style was suffocating. I thought, "How can this be? I have an open door policy. They all have stock options and access to the board and the system." I thought I was doing everything right. Resisting the initial urge to fire them all and start over, I sought out our organizational behavior consultant to explain the results. She said, "All of your direct reports love working for you and respect you, but you are too close. You have set up, and in most cases run, every department. Consequently, you tend to complete their sentences and look past their ideas for the department. Add to that a gregarious style and a penchant for managing by walking around, and you are too much. They need space." WOW! That was a wake-up call. As soon as she told me this, I instantly saw in my behaviors and preferences what she and the managers were saying. Knowing that I was having this effect on the organization, I first apologized and then modified my approach.

As a leader, you must consider your impact on the system and understand how your style, biases, and preferences color your view. Additionally, it is important to map out and understand these preferences in your individual employees and teams down through the organization.

There are many different assessment tools available to help you and your team understand the way you act and process information and how your team does so. Every brain is unique, and some are better adapted for certain tasks—risk tolerance, stress management, creativity, storytelling, goal setting, etc. The key is to understand your style, preferences, and those of your team because these shape your view and understanding of the system and its dynamics.

Assessment tools such as Myers-Briggs, Birkman, DISC, and others can be very powerful in revealing patterns of thought and action and blind spots in organizations. Means of thinking, such as DeBono's different colored hats, are also helpful in assessing and shaping patterns of thought.[75] Knowing your strengths and weaknesses and the style preferences of your teammates is critical to having effective communication and teamwork. Similar to, and in large part driven by, our left-brain/right-brain preference, each of us has a personality type and leadership style that colors the way we behave and the way we perceive things and react, particularly in times of crisis or stress.

Note from the Field

A company lost its VP of Engineering. It was fortunate to have a terrific internal candidate who had extensive experience in both engineering and product marketing. The CEO had never worked directly with him, but he was known throughout the company to be incredibly bright and well liked. After a brief search, the company elevated him to the VP position expecting great results. After some time, however, the CEO was unimpressed. It seemed the brilliance and certitude were gone. The CEO inquired of the VP of Human Resources if she had any thoughts or perspective. She asked if he had reviewed this individual's preference assessment. The CEO had not done so since the employee was not a new hire and he had fit so well in the organization before. Upon reviewing the assessment, the CEO and VP *of HR discovered the employee in question was at the highest level for introversion. It was only through sheer determination and training that he got himself through presentations and meetings, but it was exhausting. Conversely, the CEO's style was highly extroverted. He had a habit of barging in on his staff and engaging them immediately. Exactly the behavior that would be challenging to an individual assessed as a strong introvert by the instrument they used. Upon seeing the report, the CEO modified his approach to this employee. Whenever possible, he sent an email in advance with his issues or questions and asked the VP to consider them. Within days, the brilliance was back. The VP's preference was to gather the needed information, gather himself emotionally, and then address the task.*

A simple change in management style can change a dynamic immediately. Thought and emotional leadership reveal these types of dynamics. Several businesses I have worked with publish the assessment results of all employees on the hard hats of their field workers and on the nameplates of the office workers to make sure everyone has a visual cue to guide them in their interactions.

Knowledge of your leadership type, and the biases and filters it puts on your perception of people and events and of the instinctive responses this preferred style evokes in you, is critical for you and the other leaders in the system. Knowledge of the impact your type has on your peers and subordinates and knowledge of other people's types and the implications those have on your mutual ability to communicate effectively are just as critical.

Personality types and leadership/management styles are instinctive and innate. They are very hard to change and change only slowly over time and only with sufficient awareness and training. The good news is brains *can* change. Swart, Chisholm, and Brown in *Neuroscience for Leadership* describe the plasticity of the brain to learn and acquire new skills.[76] In adults, the process has four parts:

- *Awareness.* You must first be *aware* of the need to change, hence the need for humility.
- *Attention.* Your awareness needs to lead to a new level of attention to the required change.
- *Practice.* You must practice the new skills and behaviors.

- *Relationships.* Others must see, feel, and sense the changes and see you reinforce them. Note: it helps if someone is there to hold you accountable.

Working against your preference means being acutely aware of your preference and consciously working on those areas where your preference gives you blind spots or weaknesses. Understanding this and putting it into practice may require a change in personal philosophy and mindset and the ability to work against your preference. The system and the environment it resides in will often dictate a style or type of leadership, one with which you may not be initially comfortable.

Note from the Field

A family business had experienced some very difficult times. These eventually led to the company needing a dramatic turnaround. The family CEO brought in new senior managers who could quickly right the ship. The style preference map of the senior management team consisted almost entirely of change agents, hard-driving, action-oriented leaders who drove the company back to profitability and prominence by optimizing their departments; just what the company needed. It was the correct style of leadership for the reality of the times and circumstances. However, when the times and circumstances changed, the team struggled to work collectively and to employ thought and emotional leadership. Their inclination was to jump in and immediately start to do things, to fix things. When I explained the notion of action versus thought leadership they readily admitted to being overly biased to action and being almost blind to the softer elements of the system. They had to relearn behaviors and work against their preferences. Some could not do so and sought out new turnaround opportunities where action-oriented, individual problem solving was the norm.

Here are some key learning points regarding (your) leadership style or preference:

- Different does not mean wrong. Different means different.
- Different styles often emerge or are required in different
    - ° times in the business lifecycle.
    - ° functional areas of the organization.
    - ° levels in the organization.
    - ° cultural spheres in multinational organizations.
- Balance (or knowledge of bias) is critical.
- An understanding and effective use of differences can be powerful. Look for blind spots that may hamper the team and the system's ability to see. Organizations with all one style have "blind spots" due to preference.

From Hierarchy to Holarchy: The Servant Leader Model

The fourth leadership shift is a shift from viewing the enterprise as a hierarchy to viewing it as a holarchy. You will remember from our systems tenets, that systems build naturally from the bottom up, and that the higher layers are actually in place to serve the lower layers in so much as they set the linking pins that bind all the levels together and establish the purpose. This is a very different way to view the enterprise than the traditional view, but it leads to a manifestation of Max De Pree's servant leader description of the organization.[77] From a systems-thinking perspective, this view of the enterprise looks like Figure 35.

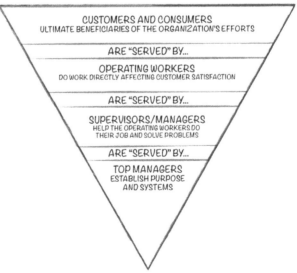

Figure 35. Servant Leader Depiction of the System

Note that viewing the system in this manner requires a change in philosophy and a change in leadership style. Humility becomes a critical attribute. Recognition by leadership of the importance and equality of the hierarchical levels is critical. Jim Collins, in his wonderful book *Good to Great*, describes leaders of this type as Level 5 leaders.[78] All the leadership levels Collins identifies are depicted in Figure 36.

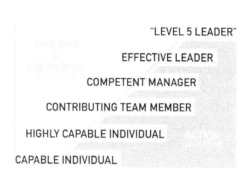

Figure 36. Level 5 Leader

Collins elaborates on the qualities that define Level 5:

> *Level 5 leaders channel their ego needs away from themselves and into the larger goal of building a great company, a great enterprise. It is not that Level 5 leaders have no ego or self-interest. Indeed, they are incredibly ambitious—but their ambition is primarily for the institution, not themselves.*[79]

As a servant leader in the system, you must make the transition

- from controlling to mentoring.
- from doing and steering to coaching and encouraging.
- from talking and directing to listening and sensing.
- from point optimization to system optimization.
- from an assemblage of individual contributors to a learning team.
- from loud leadership to quiet leadership.
- from action leadership to thought and emotional leadership.

Embrace of the Soft Systems

By now, it should be clear that systems do not operate in clear black and white, binary states. They reveal themselves in spectacular color and gray scale. Most of what you *know* about the environment the system resides in, and therefore the system, is based on assumptions and mental models of reality. In many cases, these are solid assumptions, but they are assumptions nonetheless. The final required shift in leadership thinking is the shift from a focus on the numbers to *both/ and* thinking about the numbers and the assumptions and system dynamics that produced the numbers.

Your enterprise results, the numbers, are a second-order, following effect and the result of established processes, prior decisions, and behaviors. You must look beyond the numbers to the system that produced the numbers. Remember, your enterprise is a system, perfectly designed to get the results it is getting today. So look beyond the numbers to the system and the system dynamics, with all the potential delays, to understand the numbers. Look at *both* the hard *and* the soft systems. Look at the emergent behaviors and the unintended consequences of the system, as Margaret Wheatley presents them:

We tried for many years to avoid the messiness and complexity of being human, and now that denial is coming back to haunt us. We keep failing to create outcomes and changes we need in organizations because we continue to deny that "the human element" is anything but a "soft" and not-to-be-taken-seriously minor distraction.[80]

Note from the Field

A senior leadership official for a government agency and I were at a conference on systems engineering, and our small group was discussing the future of systems engineering. I said that I believed systems engineering needed to embrace more of the soft systems skills. This individual took exception with the line of discussion and proclaimed that he did not respect the opinion of employees in his organization when they could not prove their position on a topic with solid data and statistical rigor. Approximately half the room agreed with him, proclaiming that the soft skills were not rigorous and, therefore, not to be trusted. Later that same evening, I saw the individual in question at the reception. We exchanged pleasantries, and another participant, who worked for a branch of the military and who was in our earlier session, joined us. I proceeded to ask the officer if troop morale was important to success and performance and he replied emphatically, "critical." Our *colleague heartily agreed. I then asked the officer what his unit of measure was for morale and how he knew whether it was better or worse than last time he measured it. He said, "Morale does not have a unit of measure, you have to sense it." I asked my earlier antagonist how this could be the case. How could something critical be immeasurable? He stammered a bit and replied that I clearly did not understand! Alternatively, perhaps, he does not understand and his people are paying the price.*

In the system, it is possible for an element or holon to be *both* critical to success *and* impossible to measure. One must sense the amplitude and direction. The soft systems skills are just as important as the hard systems skills, perhaps more so.

Leadership as Behavior

Leadership is hard. Management authors implore us to practice leadership, which implies we are still working on it. Authors regularly publish new models and books on leadership. To follow all of the advice dispensed you would have to be a superior species—a combination of Superman, Solomon, Mother Teresa, Wonder Woman, Patton, Rommel, Salk, Steve Jobs, Jack Welch, and many more luminaries. I know I fell short of the lofty ideal many times.

Complicating the concept further, leadership can be highly situational. The same leadership style and actions that make the CEO of a private equity-backed business successful are probably not transferable without significant modification to leading a nunnery. Some elements may be transferable, but others may not be and will need modification. That is why leadership, like all the other elements of management, must be viewed in light of the system. You must view all the elements of your enterprise management model as holons, to remind you of their systemicity, and you must tailor them to your unique situation. You must answer the question, "What should leadership look like in my enterprise, in my system?"

Jill Janov, in her book *The Inventive Organization: Hope & Daring at Work*, suggests leadership is not manifest in power, control, or direction, it is manifest in behavior.[81] The leader's behavior may reflect his or her power or need for power or control, but true leadership does not rely on them. In the system, your behavior will be the defining dynamic. No volume of words will offset your actions. The system, as a living communicating field of energy, information, and interaction, will communicate your behaviors, your actions. Occupants in the system will sense and respond to the nonverbal clues delivered with the words.

Janov's assertion begs the question, "What should those behaviors be?" My question is, "Do you have a clear model of what leadership should be in your system?" and "Do you have a common mental model of leadership for your organization?" Remember how important schema and context are to individuals. Then remember how the learning organization must have *common* mental models.

Here is a simple exercise you can conduct with your team to develop your model for leadership. Gather your team, and ask them individually to create two lists. The first list is a list of the best behaviors and traits of a leader. Ask them to think of what they believe makes a great leader. The second list is a list of the behaviors and traits of a bad leader. Ask them to list what they believe are bad leadership behaviors and traits.

Once they have completed their lists individually, ask one of the members to share one of their traits from their good list. Now ask the other attendees how many of them had the same or similar behavior. Keep this up and you will find that your team will mostly share a common view of what leadership behaviors and traits are good. Very seldom do employees tell you they admire leaders who are mean, self-absorbed, untrustworthy, and so on. The fact that there is great overlap automatically begins to build trust and consensus. Complete the exercise using the worst traits and behaviors in a similar fashion. With some discussion and editing, this exercise will yield a powerful, *common* mental model of overall leadership behaviors and traits for the leaders in the enterprise to share.

I have conducted this type of session hundreds of times over more than thirty years. The behaviors and traits given are *always* the same. You can now publish this model and train all your employees on it. You can recreate the exercise with new entrants to your system with the confidence that they will put forth leadership traits that closely align with your model.

Beware: Make sure your behaviors adhere to the model you have established and reflect what you want the system to see. The system is always on, always watching and sensing. If you espouse a set of leadership behaviors, but fail to live up to them, you will undermine your leadership.

Note from the Field

I have had a number of clients convert this exercise into a leadership rating scale, which they use during performance evaluations and in employee surveys. One client in particular turned them into continuums—Bold to Rash, and so forth—with a slider for visually showing where a leader scored, because many of the best and worst behaviors and traits are mirror images.

If you do not provide a model for leadership behaviors in your enterprise, your employees will adopt one through assimilation and accommodation. They will form the schema by default if you do not provide it by design. However, even if you provide a model, how do you live up to this model of perfection every day? The answer is, you will not live up to it at all times. You *will* violate some of these ideals. Your style will make others harder to attain and keep you from rating highly on a particular trait. You must make it clear to all that you and other leaders are not perfect, but you will strive for the ideal and make amends when you slip.

For example, I worked with a CEO who possessed many of the qualities of a great leader. However, his powerful intellect, coupled with a laserlike intensity and a terse style, led to certain friction in the company. When we examined the effect of his style on the organization, he quickly understood that he would need to modify his approach. The first step he undertook was to gather his team, acknowledge how the behaviors affected the organization, and promise to work on his interactions in the future. He ended by inviting his team to hold him to his promise. In short, he followed the steps of Swart, Chisholm, and Brown as described earlier in this chapter.

Further complicating leadership is the fact that many of the good traits are contradictory. For instance, a client had both *bold* and *contemplative* as key behaviors. We are right back to the need for *both/and* thinking. Good leadership in the system entails many seeming contradictions, for example,

- being *both* bold *and* contemplative.
- being *both* decisive *and* empathic.
- being *both* proud *and* humble.

As is often the case, Peter Drucker[82] provides the final say on leadership in the system. Drucker suggests a few simple questions a leader in the system must ask:

- Ask not "What do I want?" but "What needs to be done?"
- Then ask, "What can and should I do to make a difference?"
- Then constantly ask, "What constitutes performance and brings results in this organization?"

He adds that leaders are extremely tolerant of diversity of styles and ideas, but intolerant when it comes to performance, values, and standards. Leaders are not afraid of strong subordinates or associates. In fact, they empower them.

This leads us directly to Chapter 8 and the emergent property of the culture in the system.

Here are some things you can do, and questions you should ask, to explore and improve the leadership holon in your system:

1. Develop a shared model of leadership for your enterprise.
2. Make sure all leaders understand their leadership style and preferences and how those attributes affect the organization and the people in it.
3. Review the holon systemically. Is the purpose of leadership clear at all levels of the organization? What are the elements that make up the holon? Map out where you need leaders in the system and who your leaders are. Are the leaders' interactions healthy and supportive or detrimental?
4. Ask yourself, "How would I rate my leadership and that of others within my enterprise?" If you alone represent the leadership function in your enterprise, ask yourself, "Do I have a clear and complete view of the system? Do I have anyone to hold me accountable? Should I have a board or mentors?"

Key Takeaways
- ✓ Leadership in the system requires new roles, skills, and traits.
- ✓ Differences in leadership style and preference are powerful. Self-awareness is critical for you and your management team.
- ✓ Leaders must be trained in system thinking to see system dynamics.
- ✓ You must be both systemic and systematic, and consider both the soft and hard systems.
- ✓ You must view the system as both a hierarchy and holarchy, and practice being both leader and a servant.

✓ You must embrace both the precision and the ambiguity inherent in the system.

✓ Leadership is a behavior; model the behaviors you want to see.

Recommended Reading for Chapter 7

Bennis, Warren. *On Becoming a Leader*. Cambridge: Perseus Books, 1989. There are numerous good books available on leadership, but I think Bennis has stood the test of time. Managing in an ambiguous and changing environment is a challenge to leadership. Bennis offers great wisdom on this subject.

Bossidy, Larry, and Ram Charan. *Execution: The Discipline of Getting Things Done*. New York: Crown Business, 2002. Bossidy and Charan offer great wisdom on action leadership.

De Pree, Max. *Leadership Is an Art*. New York: Dell, 1989. De Pree's book is one of my favorites. It is short but packed with wisdom, and very approachable. He makes you feel like you are having a discussion with a trusted mentor.

Gardner, Howard. *Changing Minds*. Boston: Harvard Business School Press, 2006. Gardner's book is a great read on how we form and change our schema and mental models.

Goleman, Daniel. *Emotional Intelligence: Why It Can Matter More Than IQ*. New York: Bantam, 1995. A seminal book on the quiet leadership skill of sensing the organization.

Welch, Jack. *Winning*. New York: Harper Collins, 2005. Like Bossidy and Charan, Welch offers great wisdom on action leadership.

Chapter 8

Culture in the System

Culture is not just an ornament; it is the expression of a nation's character, and at the same time, it is a powerful instrument to mold character. The end of culture is right living.
—W. Somerset Maugham

We are caught in an inescapable network of mutuality, tied in a single garment of destiny. Whatever affects one directly, affects all indirectly.
—Martin Luther King Jr.

A s shown in Chapter 5, your enterprise system is a force field of energy and information, both of which are constantly transmitted, absorbed, and retransmitted. Your corporate culture is an *emergent property* of the system. It emerges, invisible, but powerful and pervasive, by design or by default. Occupants and new entrants can sense it immediately. It can be positive or negative. Corporate culture reflects the *totality* of the habits, beliefs, practices, values, behaviors, and actions of the enterprise and its leaders.

Each new entrant to the system will learn and assimilate the culture. As we will discuss in the next chapter on developing your people, your employees want to tap into the energy and information of the force field that is your company culture, and they will do so whether that force field is positive or negative. Culture reflects the interactions of the system and shapes the behaviors within the system. It is in large measure responsible for the level of commitment found in your employees.

Beware: There are no hard system elements of culture. You cannot measure it, and you cannot act on it directly. It is easy to talk about but elusive, powerful, and demanding. It is *both* simple *and* complex. Your culture is a story the system tells, a story that can only be understood hermeneutically. If you do not complete the story for your employees, they will complete it themselves. Your employees will make up the story, their schemata, of your culture from the experiences and behaviors they see and sense. They will read and sense it from the system.

Behold: A powerful, positive company culture is a force multiplier that emboldens all occupants and can differentiate your enterprise in this competitive world.

Values: The Foundation of Culture

> *Leadership involves conduct. Conduct is determined by values. Values are what make us who we are.*
> —H. Norman Schwarzkopf

Your values, implicit or explicit, are what form the foundation of your culture. Like purpose in the system, if values are unclear, occupants will infer them or make up the ones they believe fit the system from their viewpoint. They will view your actions and, based on those, derive the underlying values they believe inspired the action. They will infer systemic axiology. Whether you publish your values or not, the constantly communicating system that is your enterprise will transmit the values through the emergent property of culture. So what are you to do? Merely writing down the values you expect will not suffice.

Beware: There is an old Italian saying, "The paper will not refuse the ink." Values are easy to write down; living out those values is the hard part. In fact, publishing your values and then not living by them will only act as an engine of cynicism and disappointment, if not downright hypocrisy.

Note from the Field

A family business took great pains to publish its values, and constantly reminded employees how important they were to the conduct of business. Displayed conspicuously throughout the facilities, the company's values statements were a source of pride for the family. One of the prominent values for the company, and a critical safety requirement in the industry, was the prohibition on alcohol, drugs, and illegal substances. Unfortunately, one of the sons working in the business struggled with this issue. He accumulated several DWIs while using company vehicles. The mother and father kept him on the payroll in spite of these lapses. While this was beneficial for the young man, and clearly a manifestation of their love for their son, the fact that they did so eroded employees' confidence in the family values and generated widespread cynicism. The prominently displayed recitations only served to exacerbate the problem and brought into question the family's belief in, and support of, the other values they espoused.

Fortunately, you can employ a simple exercise for gaining consensus on what the values should be. Similar to the exercise in the chapter on leadership, gather your staff and ask them to write down individually the values they believe are important to them and to the business for providing guidance on behaviors. Once they have completed this exercise individually, ask one of the members to share one of their values. Now ask the other attendees how many of them had the same or similar value. Keep this up and you will find that your team will mostly share a common view of what values are important, both to them as individuals and to them as members of the enterprise. Once again, the fact that there is great overlap in values automatically begins to build trust and consensus. In the numerous times I have conducted this exercise, the values given are always the same. They speak of trust, respect, honesty, commitment, communication, compassion, etc. No individuals or teams ever propose values of sloth, hatred, mistrust, debasement, or other negative values.

There are two important derivatives from this exercise. First, once your employees have expressed their opinions as to what values are important, you can now hold them accountable to *their* values. They are no longer abstract concepts; they become personal. The employees and the system now own them. Now the values are shared values. Now there is a shared mental model of the values that are important. Second, the discussion clarifies what you mean by your values. As with the exercise on leadership, you can recreate this exercise with new entrants to your system, knowing they will closely align with your stated values. Now it is appropriate to publish your shared values.

Note from the Field

The father and founder of a family business passed away, leaving the business to his widow. A young son left his successful career in a different industry to run the company for his mother and family. The son's leadership style was very different from that of his deceased father. Where the father micromanaged and was very authoritarian in his approach, the son wanted a very open and empowering corporate culture.

We conducted the values exercise described above and, as usual, the individual values were consistent among employees and consistent with what all felt was in the best interest of the enterprise and would lead to the best corporate culture. One of the values considered most important was trust. The employees, even those with long and loyal careers at the firm, perceived the father's micromanaging and dictatorial style as a lack of trust.

Shortly after the values session, we were conducting a planning session with the same team and an old, contentious issue arose about disclosing the number of hours on bids. The supervisors felt it was critical for workers to know the number of hours bid so that employees could plan the work process. Management was concerned that employees would use all the hours in the bid even if they did not need them. It was clear to me that the long festering lack of trust was rearing its ugly head. The discussions started to become more contentious. I stopped the group and asked them to refer to the mutual values statements they had recently developed and published and explore any guidance those values might lend to the discussion. The first value on the list was trust. Upon seeing that and reflecting on their common beliefs, both sides instantly agreed they must share the information if they were to live their values.

Behold: Values are the bill of rights for your company. They establish the norms and provide the guidance for how to behave. If your values are clear and consistently upheld, people will use them in their work. They act like a keel of a boat, which provides stability and safety in rough seas. The stronger your values are, the deeper the keel will extend in the water. Strong values allow you to drive the boat harder and weather heavier seas.
Beware: You must live by your values for your employees to believe in them.

During a public session, I had a group of managers opine that if the values are clear then the decisions are easy. I asked the group if that was true, and another participant said it best. She said, "If the values are clear, the decisions are *not* any easier, they are still hard decisions, but what you *should* do is much clearer." The key is that values make it clear what you and your employees should do in certain situations. What you do becomes the defining dynamic in the system. Employees will view violations of your values as violations of trust, and they will start to erode your credibility. Because the system is always communicating and sensing, others will pick up this information, and these transmissions will begin to transform the corporate culture. Depending on the severity of the breach of trust, this erosion can be harsh and rapid. The only solution is an apology and a recommitment to the values. Not to do so will undermine the values you aspire to uphold.

Note from the Field

During one of my workshops we were conducting a values exploration session when I noticed one of the young CEOs facial expressions. I could tell he was skeptical I asked him why he looked so skeptical and if he believed in the power of values. He responded that he did believe in the power of values but he thought it tedious to list all of the proper ones. He used as an example the point I had made that employees will all give you the same values as proof of a lack of efficacy. So I asked him for his solution, which may work for you. He and his team met and published a list of things they did not like or value! He gave examples such as, sloth, lying, being rude, etc. If this approach works better for you, use it. It is your system!

How you make your values manifest in your enterprise does not matter. It is your list, make of it what you want. I know of a company that was in the process of augmenting their written values with icons to be posted in all their locations for instant recognition, and because they had a multilingual workforce.

Culture and Values as Climate

Management authors often refer to culture as setting the *climate* for the enterprise. Climate is an interesting term and leads directly to one of the most profound cultural phenomena in the system. As leaders, we have the power to bring sunshine or rain to our area of the system solely based on our style and behaviors. We can make this conscious choice, but often we do not acknowledge our part in this phenomenon.

Note from the Field

I worked with the CEO of a large manufacturing firm who struggled with mood swings. He had an immense heart and was universally beloved for his help to others. He espoused these values in his firm. However, his mood swings weighed heavily on his team. Whenever he was in the midst of these episodes, he was very hard to deal with and could be very cruel and demeaning to his staff. They had all become used to it. They felt sorry for him and wanted to help, but they felt helpless. When they saw him coming, they knew instantly whether it was going to be a good day or a bad day in the office or on the shop floor.

In my initial meeting with this CEO, he very flippantly said, "That's just the way I am," and "The staff just has to deal with it." The staff echoed this sentiment. I asked him how the team's performance was when he was in one of his moods, and he admitted it was poor. So I asked him if that was acceptable. He seemed resigned to the status quo. I asked him if he ever apologized to his staff, but he became defensive and replied, "It's just the way I am." As we explored the issue more fully, he agreed that the impact on the firm was not acceptable. His staff agreed that the behaviors were hurtful and counterproductive, but their respect for him helped them soldier on. He agreed to acknowledge the episodes with his staff and engage them in helping him deal with the negative effects. During a subsequent session, he publicly apologized for his behavior during these episodes and promised to be better. The staff wanted to believe him, but they remained skeptical.

Their skepticism was justified. During another episode, he behaved very badly and the tension was back. Sensing this, I made him gather his staff, apologize, and commit again to be more aware of his impact. It took several repetitions of this cycle before his staff finally felt justified in speaking up. The system had trained them to act a certain way, and undoing those biases took time. Eventually, the staff began to act proactively when sensing his mood through body language and tone. Bringing his staff into the process of changing his behavior had emboldened them to help him.

As time went on, he and his team became adept at sensing the climate change that was about to be visited on the office and making necessary modifications. As a symbol of this newfound openness and acceptance, I bought the office manager the Disney Grumpy and Happy dolls so that she could signal to the staff the incoming climate. Importantly, the dolls acted as a beacon to the CEO to remind him of the impact he was about to have on his team and the effect the ensuing climate would have on the system and system throughput. Seeing these reminders made him alter *his behavior, often to the extent of going to a local coffee shop and working remotely, so he would not compromise team performance.*

As a leader in the system, you must accept your impact on the culture and climate of the system. The system will reflect your values, your actions, your behaviors. Leadership's adherence to, or deviation from, established corporate values is transmitted by the system. Culture has an osmotic characteristic of permeating the enterprise and traversing all boundaries.

Culture: Hearts and Minds

Culture works in concert with purpose to connect with employees' hearts and minds. It is not enough to engage only with their minds and their personal needs. If management cannot engage hearts, the system runs the risk of being barren and soulless. We must both prescribe their environment with policies and procedures and processes, etc., and capture and inspire their hearts and minds.

Note from the Field

Many of the clients I have worked for have converted their employee manuals from a book of rules and regulation into a "user manual." Most employee manuals spend time telling employees how to get their benefits and which behaviors will result in dismissal. Trust me, most employees already know these steps. Why not give them a user manual that tells them how to succeed, behave, and excel in the system? Describe your system and the systems they will see and be a part of so they know how to relate to it and add value. Sure, tell them how to be let go as well, but at least tell them how to succeed first!

Subcultures and Subsystems

As you know, your enterprise is not monolithic. There are different styles, functions, holons, and subsystems throughout. These subsystems can and will exhibit different subcultures. There will be subcultures in accounting, sales, operations, and other divisions. These differences are to be expected, and in most cases encouraged. However, two system caveats must guide these bounded subcultures.

1. First, your values are what traverse the boundaries and are universal to the whole system. The values in the various subsystems and departments must be consistent with overall values or else different areas of the system will begin to behave differently with regard to values.
2. Second, you must be vigilant about bounded rationality. Departments and subcultures will naturally want to begin to optimize around their specialty or boundaries.

Signs of Cultural Trouble

Signs that an enterprise's culture is in trouble will be readily apparent and constantly transmitted due to the connectedness of the system. Deal and Kennedy in *Corporate Culture* cite the following signs:[83]

✓ There is a lack of clarity about the purpose, values, and beliefs of the enterprise. This lack of clarity soon has the organization working at cross-purposes, leading to entropy.

✓ There is a lack of agreement on what is important to attain success. This lack of agreement leads directly to multifinality and conflicting efforts.

✓ Disorganized day-to-day activities and interactions further divide the organization, leading to frustration and blame.

✓ Diverse fundamental beliefs among subunits lead to harmful bounded rationality.

✓ Often, destructive or disruptive heroes emerge; employees who accomplish heroic feats, but who fail to build a common understanding of what is important for the system.

Unfortunately, this is the state of many enterprises today. For decades, the Gallup organization has surveyed organizations for levels of employee engagement. In 2014, approximately 30 percent of those surveyed indicated they were "actively engaged" at their work; 51 percent indicated they were "not engaged"; and 19 percent responded they were "actively disengaged."[84] In the vast majority of companies, more than half the employees are disengaged. They do not know how they are supposed to add value, where they fit in, what constitutes performance, how to advance, and as a consequence, they do not respect management.

Knowing what you now know about systems, you should realize that your system drives most of the behaviors, and you cannot escape your role in creating those behaviors. You constructed the system, or let it develop by default, and you chose the occupants.

This leads us directly to the next common holon; the selection and development of your most important asset—your people.

Here are some things you can do, and questions you should ask, to explore and improve the culture holon in your system:

1. Are you clear about the values at work in your organization? If you are, have you published them?
2. Engage your employees actively in developing, refining, and preserving your values.
3. Are you and your team, especially leaders in the system, adhering to them? If not, are there consequences?
4. Are you allowing employees, especially key performers, to violate your company values, thereby eroding the values in the eyes of other employees? Remember, the other employees will see, or hear about the violations, and they will wonder why you do not act.

Key Takeaways
- ✓ Culture is a powerful system force and dynamic.
- ✓ You cannot control culture directly—it emerges from the system.
- ✓ Values are the underlying foundation of culture.
- ✓ Culture is directly related to, and stems from, leadership and leader's actions.
- ✓ Live by your values. You must act out your values. Actions, not words transmit the values.
- ✓ Enforce your values. You must remove or marginalize destructive elements that countermand your values.
- ✓ Hire for your values. You can train for skills, but values are internal to each individual.

Recommended Reading for Chapter 8
Douglas, Mary. *How Institutions Think*. Syracuse, NY: Syracuse University Press, 1986.

Gardner, Howard. *Changing Minds*. Boston: Harvard Business School Press, 2006.

Goleman, Daniel. *Emotional Intelligence: Why It Can Matter More Than IQ*. New York: Bantam, 1995.

Pink, Daniel H. *Drive: The Surprising Truth about What Motivates Us* (New York: Riverhead Books, 2011. Culture is a key driver of motivation. *Drive* revisits much of what we know about what motivates people and employees.

Sinek, Simon. *Start with Why*. New York: Penguin, 2009. Without a compelling why, it is hard to build a powerful corporate culture.

Chapter 9

Employee Learning and Development in the System

What I've learned over many years, especially at Motorola, is
that management makes a mistake in not expecting enough,
not realizing how much people can really do. If you set high
expectations, it's almost a compliment to good people.
—George Fisher

don't believe it is almost a compliment, I believe it *is* a compliment to good people to expect a lot from them. I believe doing so says, "I trust and believe in you." As with our other chapters, I am not going to recite all of the good advice you have read from the assembled writing on employee development. In this chapter, we are going to explore how taking a systems approach may change your approach to employee development.

Virtually every owner, CEO, executive director, or manager will say that employees are their most important asset. Yet very few enterprises outside of large multinational corporations actually take a systematic approach to selecting and developing this asset. Employee development is too often solely comprised of group training, or developing certain localized skills and behaviors to optimize portions of the system—a department, team, or individual.

While these efforts are important, they can lead to a systematization of bounded rationality. By training only in parts of the system, or certain processes, you may inadvertently send the message that the parts are the focus. To avoid this, you need to develop employees' competence in *both* the system *and* their individual competence.

In this chapter, we will explore the following key elements of employee development as it relates to your system:

1. We will explore the need to teach your system. If you did not know about systems thinking before reading this book, your employees almost certainly do not.
2. We will look at the difference between training and development.
3. We will explore giving our employees all-important systems context and how this context will box employees into their holon, giving them a clear part in the system in which to shine.
4. Finally, we will look at delegation, the essence of development.

Teach the System

You cannot lose sight of the need to teach the system, the whole, as well as the parts. In your system, learning and development are about growing the capabilities of every element of the system—employees, processes, machines, software— while keeping it aligned with the purpose and assuring that the quality of the interactions grow as well. The employees, processes, subsystems, *and* the system as a whole must grow and develop *together*. Remember, as a system, they are inseparable. Your employees must develop *in conjunction* with the whole system.

Sharing the models of your Enterprise Management System (as shown in Figure 37) begins to give your employees the systems-thinking context. The EMS gives

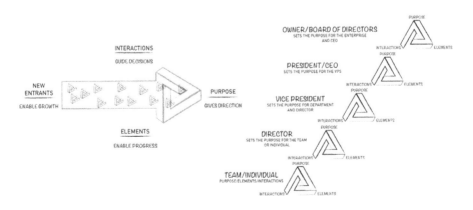

Figure 37. Enterprise Management System Models

them a complete picture of the overall system. Employees will see the common management elements at work and understand how the holons replicate down through the enterprise with appropriate adaptation at the subsystem level—department, team, project, and individual.

Employees must see the how the system, in which they are working, operates. Imagine how you would feel if you could not see critical parts of your system. Prior management literature has characterized this feeling as bowling with a curtain covering the pin opening. Your boss tells you to bowl a strike. You dutifully roll the ball towards the pins and wait expectantly for the crash of pins. However, you cannot see the result because of the curtain. Your boss comes up to you and says, "That wasn't very good. I am disappointed, now step up and get that spare." How can you bowl a spare if you do not know which pins remain? Without system context and mental models, your employees will be similarly challenged. Your employees must have a view of the system in which they reside. They must have proper system context.

Corporate universities of large established companies exist to do just this. Disney, Dow, GE, Heineken, Prudential, Siemens, Toyota, and many more, all have corporate universities. I do not think it is a coincidence that these companies rank among the most admired and successful companies, and are the subjects of many management books. While many do not explicitly teach systems thinking, a mistake in my opinion, they exist to impart common system knowledge—purpose, vision, values, beliefs, language, mental models, practices, processes, and policies—to all occupants of the system. These institutions exist to enable Senge's learning organization, by building common views and models of the system—building *shared mental models*.

Owners, CEOs, and non-profit executive directors of smaller entities often assume they cannot afford to implement such a construct. I want to challenge you on this assumption. According to Training Industry, Inc., on average, large multinational corporations spend between 0.5 percent and 1.2 percent of revenue on employee development.[85] Given these numbers, a pizza parlor with $300,000 in revenue would have to spend $1,200–3,600 to provide comparable development resources. This could come in the form of providing your team with copies of this book, reading it together, and jointly discussing and developing your system models. It might entail group video viewing and discussions on key topics or establishing a shared library. If you are talking about your most important asset, shouldn't you make this small investment?

You do not have to have a majestic facility, which looks like a college campus. You simply have to invest the time to provide your employees with the mental models of the whole system as well as the models of their parts. I have worked with a number of companies who have set up their own corporate universities to teach the concepts contained in this book. In the recommended reading for this chapter, I have listed a book on setting up a corporate university, *The Corporate University Handbook*, which provides guidance on this task.

Develop, Rather than Train, Employees

> *Training is for animals, development is for our employees.*
> —Louis Charles (Charlie) Roudane[86]

Charlie, a CEO and consultant I worked with for years, used that line in our sessions with owners and presidents. He used the provocative line to draw attention to the critical need for viewing your employees as assets to *be developed*, not automatons to be perfected or animals to be trained for a performance. We often provide training with an implied asymmetrical nature. Even our language bespeaks this. We say, "We have to train everyone in X," or "Send Sally to training on Y," rather than "Our frontline employees need better customer service skills," and then providing the training for them to develop their skills and capabilities.

Learning is a reflexive verb. You cannot "learn" anybody anything! *They* must learn the material, the concept, or the skill for themselves. We often force people to go to training or mass train our employees, but we have no idea whether they learned anything or developed better habits, skills, perspective, or understanding. Development is about the latter. Development is about broadening your employee's perspectives and enhancing their ability to impart their energy and knowledge to the system.

You must adopt a philosophical shift from *training* your employees to *developing* them, which may include training. You must make sure your employees are actually learning and developing the skills required, not just for the job, but also for the system. If you only train them in the job, they may dutifully perform, but not know why they are doing the task.

As stated before, the Gallup survey has found that in the vast majority of companies, more than half the employees are disengaged. I believe a major contributor to these findings is the fact that most companies do not reveal the system to their employees. Most companies do not complete the hermeneutic circle for their employees, leaving them seeing only the parts, not the whole. Consequently, their employees are disoriented. They have not become oriented to their environment, the system. They see only the parts or their own part. Hermeneutically, they cannot complete the story.

Training is a critical function, but it is about creating new skills and competencies within each individual. *Development* is the process of completing the story for them. Development is about creating a system holon, which is a powerful, directed element of the system, connected to purpose, reflective of the shared values, and able to deliver the needed throughput by virtue of high-quality interactions. Development is about engaging your employees in the purpose of the enterprise.

Many managers think engagement is talking to their employees, but it is a far greater concept. Engaged employees sense a real connection to the information and the energy of the system and the purpose of the system. Remembering that context can enhance learning and comprehension by 50–100 percent, you must give employees context for *both* the part of the system they play a role in *and* the whole system.

The Development Continuum

In order to make the mental shift from training to developing, it is important to understand the learning and development continuum your employees are traversing as they develop new competencies and capabilities. The development continuum dovetails with a process of learning called Hebbian learning. In Hebbian learning, as described by Swart, Chisolm, and Brown,[87] an individual employee traverses through the following path as they learn and develop new skills and capabilities:

- *Executive function.* This is something you do. You execute a task, but if you have never done it before, you may struggle to learn it. The steps, actions, and language will all feel foreign.
- *Memory.* As you learn, you remember certain elements, patterns and steps, which enhance your ability to learn.
- *Habit.* The accumulation of knowledge and experience begins to convert the practice to habit.
- *Embodied knowledge.* The knowledge is a part of you and becomes instinctive.

Hebbian learning parallels the four stages of competence developed by Noel Burch,[88] which, with the following descriptions of the developmental process, make up a knowledge continuum that spans from a novice to an expert (see Figure 38).

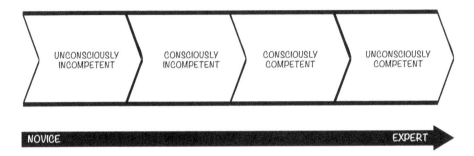

Figure 38. Knowledge Continuum

Below are the learning elements your employees are struggling with during the stages:

- *Unconsciously incompetent.* They have no knowledge or experience with *their* new reality demanded by the new reality of the enterprise. They do not know they are incompetent. In fact, they probably think they are competent at their current job, which makes the next stage that much more jarring.
- *Consciously incompetent.* Now they have knowledge of the need to learn, but little ability to make an impact on implementation. This is a very uncomfortable stage. During this phase, there might be anger, denial, and the accompanying emotional strain, none of which enhance the learning condition.
- *Consciously competent.* This stage is characterized by an acute focus on materials. Employees will be reliant on a specific sequence or plan. Application of the new learning is dependent on feedback and supervision. This stage is very mechanistic. As employees develop in this stage, the need to focus on materials, plans, and sequence go down. They extract concepts and relations by themselves and no longer need strict adherence to sequence. Employees can apply the learning across context and the need for supervision decreases dramatically.
- *Unconsciously competent.* By this stage, employees have clear mental models and a connection of knowledge to practice. They can adapt knowledge and practice to different situations, and no supervision is required.

As you can see from these descriptions, what appears to be a simple process of training someone is in fact a very complex and emotional continuum, a process that requires time, empathy, and patience. As a leader and manager, you have to *sense* where each employee is on the continuum in order to assure your employee is developing along it.

Their Part of the System: Boxing Employees In

Once you provide a view of the overall system, you need to provide your employees context for their area of the system, for their holon. Your employees need to know certain key inputs for them to orient themselves to their system role. In order for your employees to actively engage, you must show them

✓ where they fit in the overall system.
✓ what you expect them to do in the system.
✓ how they add value in the system.
✓ how they are supposed to act in the system.

Figure 39 shows the many key inputs your employees must have to understand fully their part in the system. Understanding all of the inputs to their holon, and the total system, the parts and the whole, is critical to achieving the personal mastery of the system.[89]

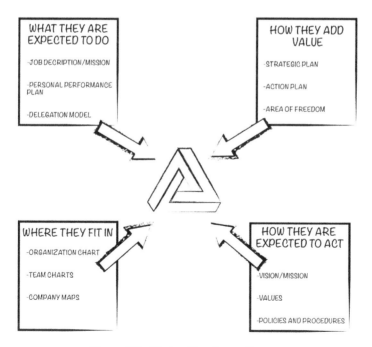

Figure 39. Giving Employees Context

Boxing Employees In

> *Give them a box that they don't fear and*
> *let them perform within it and let them grow it.*
> —Jack Welch

You will note that the graphic in Figure 39 appears to box employees into their holon. This is precisely what is happening in the system. By default, their holon has boundaries. It must, for it cannot extend forever in all directions. Yet most managers do not adequately describe these boundaries for their employees. People need and want to know their boundaries as this note from the field reveals.[90]

Note from the Field

An El-High (combined elementary through high school) had the elementary school housed in a corner of a larger school complex. The elementary school had access to a small outside playground surrounded by a wire mesh fence, with playground equipment in the center. The playground was in the midst of all of the other athletic fields used by the school. The elementary grade students were released in the morning and ran all over the area, often climbing on the fence and challenging the boundaries. The school administration noticed this phenomenon and noted that the elementary students were out for recess when the rest of the school was engaged in the classrooms. Not wanting to restrict the freedoms of the students, they suggested removing the fence that separated the playground from the larger playing fields. It was agreed that this was prudent, and the fencing was removed.

Then something interesting happened. When the students were first released into the new play area, the vast majority of them cautiously congregated near the doors to the school and did not even venture out as far as they had when the fences were in place! When asked about this phenomenon, the students who did not range out *replied that they were scared and unsure what they could do and where they could go. The fence had provided clear guidance, and they felt free to run right up to it. The fence provided a clear boundary, which delineated their safe area. They felt free to run and play as hard as they wanted within this safe area. Counterintuitively, they were free in the confined area and felt less free in the open area. Conversely, one or two intrepid students immediately headed for places they probably shouldn't have been and needed the fence to keep them from harm.*

Your employees want to, and need to, know their boundaries. If they do not know where the boundaries are, either they will make them up based on their own risk profile or they will expand them beyond what may be prudent, as the anecdote revealed. Both are suboptimal. The need to understand our boundaries is universal. Employee empowerment without corresponding boundaries can be frightening. Giving employees the needed context means mutually defining the boundaries that are safe and expected, and letting them run as hard and as free in them as possible. This is another one of our *both/and* simplexities. The employees must be *both* bounded *and* free.

As an exercise, take your current organization chart, and review, employee by employee, whether you have provided your direct reports with clear guidance on all the inputs shown in Figure 39. You may be surprised at how little you have actually told your employees about your system and the area your employee occupies. If this is the case, start having those conversations. You will be surprised what you find out. It has been my experience that most managers do not really know their employees' real capabilities, fears, strengths, and weaknesses. It is critical for each of you to have an understanding of these in order to delegate authority and responsibility appropriately. Once you have completed the exercise at your level, systematize the process by having your direct reports conduct the same exercise with their employees.

Behold: The simple process of conducting the conversations described above is the essence of development and can unleash potential within your employees, previously locked away, unavailable to the system.
Beware: Although the process is simple, the complexity comes from the nature of the discussions. You will be talking about people's livelihoods and

competencies and these reflect self-worth. As a manager and a leader, you, along with your employee, have to learn to conduct these discussions.

Delegation

Delegation and entrusting employees is one of the hardest areas for many owners, CEOs, and managers to master. For the enterprise to thrive and grow, however, you must develop these capabilities. If not you do not develop them, the system will suffer, and it will be a result of your failings, not the employees.

Note from the Field

I was conducting a public session with about thirty owners and presidents. We were covering the topics in this chapter, and an owner was becoming increasingly dismissive and agitated. I sensed this and asked him to share his frustrations with the group. He proceeded to tell the group that the techniques we were espousing would never work in his company. When I asked him why not, he responded because he could not trust his employees and therefore could not delegate to them. A fellow attendee jumped in and asked him why he hired employees he could not trust and told him he needed to work on his hiring practices. The owner stammered and replied that he had not hired people he could not trust. At that point, another owner jumped in and pointed out that if he initially hired trustworthy employees and now they were untrustworthy, then he needed to look at his management development practices, as they were not working. Either way, this leader was the architect of the system in question, and there was no escaping the system results. It took the individual in question a while to calm down, but later in the session he acknowledged that his hiring and development processes both needed extensive work.

In the last section, we described a contextual box for your employee, which provides them with clarity and specificity about their role in the system. Tannenbaum and Schmidt call this box an employee's area of freedom.[91] As Figure 40 below indicates, your employee's area of freedom relates inversely to your use of authority. As we discussed in Chapter 7 on leadership, your title and position grant you certain authority within the enterprise. As Jill Janov suggested in *The Inventive Organization*, your leadership is not manifest in this authority; it is manifest in your behavior. If you use your authority to direct, control, and micromanage your direct reports, you will stifle them.

Figure 40. Leadership Continuum

To become an effective leader in the system you must let go; give clear guidance in direction; establish clear, mutual expectations; and communicate clearly the boundaries of the environment but not methods and actions within. In short, as the leader, you must delegate. It is the critical interaction of transferring purpose, information, and passion between holarchic layers of the system. If you have chosen your employees well, and fail to do this, the employees will view the lack of delegation as a lack of trust.

Balancing Competency and the Area of Freedom

As a leader, you must balance both the need for boundaries and the need for freedom. As can be seen in Figure 41, the employee's area of freedom must relate to the individual's competency within that area.[92] Too large an area of freedom without corresponding competence can lead to timidity, self-doubt, and mistakes of competency.

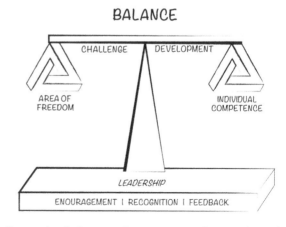

Figure 41. Balancing Competency and Area of Freedom

You should not cede authority to those who are not yet ready to accept it. However, too small an area of freedom for accomplished, capable employees will feel restrictive and controlling.

Confucius correctly gauged this dynamic long ago:

> *The superior man is easy to serve and difficult to please. If you try to please him in any way which is not accordant with right, he will not be pleased. But in his employment of men he uses them according to their capacity. The inferior man is difficult to serve, and easy to please. If you try to please him, though it be in a way not accordant with right, he may be pleased. But in his employment of men he wishes them to be equal to everything.*[93]

You must construct each area of freedom *individually* and in concert with your employee. You cannot grant the same area of freedom to employees who have differing levels of competency. You have to understand where each employee is on the continuum of development and competency.

Discussing and negotiating the boundaries clearly and concisely establishes a mutual understanding of expectations and sets the scene for the delegator to turn over authority to the delegate and for the delegate to accept responsibility and accountability for the described area. The conditions must be clear to both parties. As a manager, you cannot *give* someone accountability or responsibility. Your employee must reciprocate, and *accept* them. Authority to act, accountability, and responsibility are inexorably linked.

> **Beware:** Many employees want more authority to act, but are unwilling to accept the corresponding responsibility and accountability.

Many employees want the higher pay and authority without the attendant responsibility and accountability. As De Pree writes, "Opportunity must always be connected to accountability. Without true opportunity and risk, there is no chance to seize accountability" [and vice versa].[94] Conversely, the manager must release authority or remain responsible and accountable. Only this mutual exchange builds trust. This trust must exist on many levels.

Note from the Field

The owner of a large equipment rental company struggled with trusting his employees. He had a hard time letting go of simple details with respect to his employees, even those with many years of service. His controller was trying to implement a purchase card program for fuel and incidental expenses to facilitate jobs in the field. The owner struggled with the idea of giving his employees a p-card and letting them obligate the company without oversight. I asked him if he was on every job site, every minute of every job, and he dismissively said "of course not." The controller and I proceeded to point out that if that was the case, then a typical crane operator was already being trusted with the owner's $300,000 crane, a client's $250,000 boiler, and a client relationship with the general contractor that probably ran into the millions of dollars. It seemed counterproductive not to trust a twenty-year employee with a $150 limit p-card! Viewed in this light, the owner relented and agreed that it did not make much sense.

Beware and Behold: The dynamics of your marketplace dictate that change will be a constant in your life as a manager and the lives of your employees (see Chapter 14, "Change and the System"). Consequently, the development of your people will be a constant. There will be opportunities to change and grow. This does not always mean in stature and rank in the company. Some employees may not want to rise in rank or take on more responsibility. This is acceptable as long as they continue to grow and learn in their chosen roles. Growth and personal mastery in one's current role should be expected and encouraged. However, staying in the same role implies their pay may only rise with cost of living increases or market rates.

Delegation is critical to enhance the power and direction of each holon in the system. Remember the simple enterprise equation from Chapter 3, which states, our results are the sum of all the individual results. Without the critical interaction and the exchange of authority, responsibility, and accountability inherent in delegation there remains only one person responsible and accountable, the manager, and the employee area of freedom shrinks. Under these circumstances, system throughput, results, will be suboptimized.

Wheatley describes how delegation optimizes the whole system:

> *In organizations, if people are free to make their own decisions, guided by a clear organizational identity for them to reference, the whole system develops a greater coherence and strength.*[95]

From this greater strength and freedom, both the system and the employee can grow. Each holon grows in capability and commitment, and the force field that is the enterprise becomes more powerful. However, the leader must balance this freedom given to the employee with acceptance of responsibility and the competence and capability to accept and accomplish the task.

Delegation: The Process

The most powerful technique for effective delegation is to have simple, straightforward discussions with all employees about the key inputs that define their holon and area of freedom as described in Figure 39. One of the great benefits of these sessions is the rich engagement that occurs in doing so. Employees feel valued and respected, and management can learn a great deal about the employees. Together you can complete the hermeneutic circle and surface many surprising assumptions. Making sure everyone is oriented to the system and their role in it is critical and can be very rewarding, and yet, most managers do not conduct these discussions. Absent these discussions, there will be no closure to the circle and agreement on mutual expectations.

You will note that the above discussions require certain preexisting conditions. The manager must begin with a clear idea of the purpose, values, plans, jobs, structure, and beliefs of the system in order to conduct these discussions (see Chapters 8 through 10 for more information on these inputs to the area of freedom). To have the area of freedom discussions described above, it is imperative to create many of the key system inputs with which to describe the area of freedom. As Deming, Drucker, Senge, Wheatley, and a multitude of others have reported, the absence of these fundamental system inputs is responsible for most management and employee frustration and failure. By simply conducting adult conversations about these inputs, you can build important system capabilities; trust and employee engagement.

> **Beware:** While simple, delegation conversations are anything but easy. They are made complex by the number and importance of the inputs and by the personal nature of the discussions. Additionally, they get to the value and self-worth of individuals. Ignoring these discussions sends the message that you feel your people are not worthy of the discussion. If you do not conduct these discussions, your employees will complete the story themselves to complete the hermeneutic circle.
> **Behold:** These simple conversations can unleash the power and passion inherent in individuals and make them available to the system.

Company Areas of Freedom

Just as an individual needs a safe, prescribed area of freedom to be effective, so do the hierarchical levels of the enterprise. If the individual areas of freedom are small, by extension, the organization collapses on itself. Enterprises with an abundance of autocratic managers not only suffer from restricted individual areas of freedom, but the entire organization can feel suffocating and closed. Figure 42 demonstrates such an organization. There is insufficient space between hierarchical levels due to poor delegation, feedback, communication, and a corresponding lack of trust. Enterprises like this are typically practicing bounded rationality within the various departments and functional areas and reflect the barren, psychic prisons described in the management literature by Wheatley, Douglas, and Gardner.

Leadership's ability to delegate and establish clear areas of freedom frees up management to pursue more strategic actions (see Figure 43). Additionally,

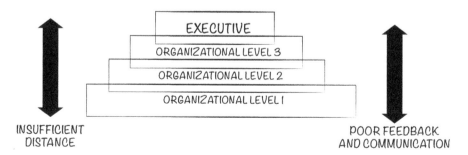

Figure 42. Compressed Hierarchy

Figure 43. Expanded Hierarchy

employees enjoy greater job satisfaction and are more engaged in such an enterprise. System throughput is dramatically improved. I have had owners and managers tell me they feel they have regained upwards of 30 percent of their time just from focusing on the critical *interaction* of defining a clear area of freedom and imparting clear direction on purpose.

Finally, a similar type of compression can occur departmentally or laterally in the organization. This type of compression usually is a result of managers at certain levels of the enterprise not effectively sharing information and resources critical to the system. This results in the classic silo depiction of a dysfunctional organization.

Here are some things you can do, and questions you should ask, to explore and improve the learning and development holon in your system:

1. Develop the system models of your enterprise and share them with your employees.
2. Show each employee where he or she fits in your system.
3. Develop all of the inputs necessary to describe an area of freedom.
4. Develop your model of the area of freedom. Share the model and the process of discussing with each manager and employee.
5. Conduct the area of freedom discussions with all your direct reports and have them do the same with their direct reports.

Key Takeaways

✓ Development of your people is more than training. It is about connecting to purpose and engaging the whole individual.

✓ All occupants must be allowed to develop both systems thinking and individual skills.

✓ Leadership must give context at both the system level and the holon level.

✓ Leadership must define an area of freedom that is both freeing and confining.

✓ Leadership must choose wisely and continuously assess fit with the area of freedom.

Recommended Reading for Chapter 9

Allen, Mark. *The Corporate University Handbook*. New York: AMACOM, 2002.

Bennis, Warren. *On Becoming a Leader*. Cambridge: Perseus Books, 1989.

Bossidy, Larry, and Ram Charan. *Execution: The Discipline of Getting Things Done*. New York: Crown Business, 2002.

Collins, James C., and Jerry I. Porras. *Built to Last: Successful Habits of Visionary Companies*. New York: Harper Business, 1994.

Collins, James C. *Good to Great: Why Some Companies Make the Leap and Others Don't*. New York: Harper Collins, 2001.

De Pree, Max. *Leadership Is an Art*. New York: Dell, 1989.

Drucker, Peter F. *The Essential Drucker*. New York: Harper, 2001.

Cotter, John, P. *Leading Change*. Boston: Harvard Business School Press, 1996.

Gardner, Howard. *Changing Minds*. Boston: Harvard Business School Press, 2006.

Goleman, Daniel. *Emotional Intelligence: Why It Can Matter More Than IQ*. New York: Bantam, 1995.

Jick, Todd D. *Managing Change: Cases and Concepts*. Boston: Irwin, 1993.

Kohn, Alfie. *Punished by Rewards*. New York, Houghton Mifflin, 1993.

Medina, Jon. *Brain Rules*. Seattle: Pear Press, 2014.

Pink, Daniel H. *Drive: The Surprising Truth about What Motivates Us*. New York: Riverhead Books, 2011.

Sinek, Simon. *Start with Why*. New York: Penguin, 2009.

Chapter 10

Planning in the System

If you fail to plan, you are planning to fail.
—Benjamin Franklin

A s emphasized in the previous chapter, one of the key benefits of an effective system for the development of your people is to connect them to the purpose of the enterprise, to engage them fully in the enterprise. In the system, the critical function of the planning process is not the development of a specific plan. The plan is merely an artifact of the planning process. The most important part of the planning process is the strategic discussions that create and drive the plan. As Peter Senge points out, planning is a form of "institutional learning" that enables enterprises to continually adapt and grow. He describes the planning process thusly:

> *. . . the process whereby management teams change their shared mental models of the company, their markets, and their competitors. For this reason we think of planning as learning and of corporate planning as institutional learning.*[96]

Christopher Bartlett and Sumantra Ghoshal in *Beyond Strategy to Purpose* write about precisely this use for the planning process. They encourage management to use the planning process to build a rich engaging purpose. Describing how great companies use the systems-thinking approach and techniques we have been discussing, the authors write:

> *First, they place less emphasis on following a clear strategic plan than on building a rich, engaging corporate purpose. Next, they focus less on formal structural design and more on effective management processes. Finally, they are less concerned with controlling employees' behavior than with developing their capabilities and broadening their perspectives.*[97]

We saw in Chapter 3 the critical importance of the interaction level to level in the system where purpose is imparted from the higher holon to the lower holon. This is the critical step. People connect with purpose, not sales figures or market share. As you read in the prior chapter on employee development, your employees need the context for what you are asking them to do. They need to know how they align with the purpose and the plan. Absent this, they will either act boldly on their own objectives or timidly creep hoping they will achieve clarity along the way.

To build this type of engagement, you must do three critical things:

1. First, you must share the planning process.
2. Next you must revisit your prior assumptions and look past all of the biases and filters they may have created in your current system.
3. Finally, you must drive the decisions you make, and the information that drove them, down through the organization.

Sharing the Planning Process

In order to develop an effective system, all of the elements of the system have to share common information, common processes, and common mental models. This is the only way to build shared mental models and a shared purpose. To do this, you need to adopt team-based planning.

Team-Based Planning

The place to start is with your planning process. As we discussed in Chapter 4, the most common holons that make up your management system are already at play in your enterprise. Consequently, you currently have a planning process. The question then becomes "Is it an effective process?"

Note from the Field

I had the discussion on an effective planning process with the owner of a medium-sized enterprise some years ago. He remarked that he did not have, or need, a planning process; he just decided what he was going to do and told his employees what to do from there. When I asked him how he decided what to do, he replied that he considered what the economy was going to do, and what prices for commodities were going to do. He said he talked with other business owners about market trends and how customer needs and wants were changing. He said he explored employment data and many, many other inputs. Armed with all of the inputs, he considered them and decided what he would do. He would then tell his employees what they were supposed to do when the time came for them to do it. I said, "See, you do have a planning process."

The problem with our friend above is he is the only one in his system who knows the process, the assumptions he made in the process and the rationale for the decisions. When he subsequently delivered to his employees their tasks associated with his plan, the tasks were lacking all of the system intelligence his employees needed to be truly engaged and successful. All his employees had were pieces of the story, a limited set of models, and no rationale for the actions they were being asking to take. They could not see if there was an integrated pattern of actions chosen in response to the environment, so they were left to wonder why they are to take the actions. They were powerless to act on anything except their owner's instruction. Finally, the owner has denied his employees the opportunity to shape their own destiny and perhaps help the owner with his decisions. This condition is safe for the owner, but stultifying for competent employees. In short, they had a small, ill-defined area of freedom. The owner's system for planning produced the perfect conditions of a soulless, psychic prison. A prison which is perfectly designed to get the results it is getting—disengaged employees.

Choosing Your Planning Process

There is a multitude of resources available to managers anxious to tailor a planning process to their system, and I commend those to you in the Recommended Reading section. However, you have already seen a great initial model for planning—the OODA loop. Essentially, all strategic planning models incorporate some version of Boyd's model.

1. *Observe.* Deeply and critically observe your external and internal environments.
2. *Orient.* Orient yourself to the realities of your external and internal environments—essentially establishing the opportunities and threats inherent in the external environment, and the strengths and weaknesses of your organization with respect to the internal environment.
3. *Decide.* Given the information above, decide what your response is going to be—refine your purpose, vision, mission as needed and develop your plan.
4. *Act.* In accordance with the plan, delegate tasks to department, teams, and individuals so they can act according to the plan.

The first step is to make a critical assessment of the external environment (Drucker's basis for the first set of assumptions in your business theory), and review and restate your key assumptions. In my experience, most entities and their management teams do not dig deep enough and do not know their environments well enough. Similar to managers listening with their response track in their head waiting to deliver it rather than listening, management teams study the markets and the external environment looking to find what fits their wants, their filters, and their comfort zone. Additionally, by including your employees in this exploration you derive three benefits: greater understanding of the environment, greater understanding of the rationale for the ensuing plan, and greater commitment to that plan.

Similarly, most managers and management teams are not critical enough of their internal situation and do not know their system and system results well enough. Here again, including your employees in an honest assessment of your current assumptions, system, policies, and processes builds greater engagement.

Beware: The external market and environment do not care about your system and your needs. The external world does not care about your internal constraints or personal desires. Markets, customers, regulators, and others reveal needs and wants and wait for enterprises to bring solutions and satisfiers. You need to become relentlessly curious about the external world, adopting the mindset of being outwardly focused and market driven. **Behold:** Enterprises that are willing to listen, observe, and then adapt their systems to the market needs can be handsomely rewarded.

Note: Referring back to our discussions in Chapter 7 on types of thinking and management styles, during the observation phase, right-brain thinkers can help left-brain thinkers see patterns and make connections, and lefts can use their analytical skills on the data. In the internal phase left-brain thinkers can drive the linear process of planning while the rights help with thinking outside the box for creative solutions to capture opportunities and solve internal challenges. This is another reason why it is critical for leaders to understand these type and style differences and to embrace them. During the planning process there are distinct phases—exploration and then execution planning. Right-brain types are better and more comfortable during the exploration phase, and left-brain types are better at execution planning.

Revisit Your Assumptions

A key technique during the observation phase is the ability to step outside the enterprise and view it dispassionately without the filters and biases as depicted in Figure 44. Management has to be very aware of the biases, philosophies, and underlying assumptions that drive current thought and frame current mental models about the external and internal environment. Remember, your system and your current mental models shape your viewpoint.

The Importance of Viewpoint

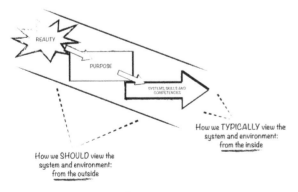

When you view the system from a position within the system, an enormous number of filters and biases and prior assumptions affect your view. You must mentally step outside of the system and use a new set of lenses provided by systems thinking to view the system clearly. The language of lenses is not accidental on my part. How you view

Figure 44. Viewpoint of the Enterprise

the system, and where you stand when you view the system, determine what you see. You must revisit the fundamental assumptions that are the foundation of the business and verify their appropriateness. Practically, this is very hard to do, and the implications seen from this view can be hard to face emotionally. However, just because something is hard or emotional does not excuse management from addressing it. One thing is certain: whatever you see will persist whether you address it or not.

> **Beware:** The system is always communicating, and it disperses these fundamental assumptions throughout the enterprise and stores them deep in the collective psyche.

Suspending systematic and personal biases—viewing the system environment with fresh eyes—is critical to being able to make the necessary changes as dictated by the reality. It is a critical part of the process of keeping the system poised for positive change, balanced on the knife-edge of dynamic equilibrium as shown in Figure 20. Remember, your employees assume you set up the current system and you have developed them to perform, at whatever level, in the current system. If in observing the external or internal environment, you become uncomfortable and determine change is needed, you must share the reasons. All of the occupants of the system must see the need for change. If not, they will rightfully fight for the status quo. After all, you have told them to prepare for the status quo. You have designed the system to be good at the status quo. Absent making the need for change visible, system occupants will fight to keep the system whole. As Todd Jick said, to get them to change you must get them as uncomfortable as you are with the status quo.

Looking beyond the Numbers

As described in Chapter 7, leaders and managers must also remember the admonition to look beyond just the numbers in the plan. In fact, the numbers can become a major obstacle. Remember that the numbers are a *result* of the system throughput and may be clouded by long delays and shaped by system dynamics. Management must look at both the numbers and the system that spawned the numbers.

Many owners and managers are reluctant to provide this level of transparency and share operating and financial information so widely. I encourage you to overcome this reluctance. Jack Stack, in *The Great Game of Business*, writes that the damage done by not revealing this information is far greater to the enterprise in terms of trust, knowledge, and resulting performance than any competitive threats.[98]

Note from the Field

I worked with a family business that was trying to professionalize its management and planning processes. The owner's husband had died, leaving her in charge. During our sessions, we discussed many of the techniques in this book, and I suggested sharing the company's results with the employees during the planning sessions and throughout the year. At first, the owner was very reluctant to do so. She was a very private person, and she and her husband had never shared the results before. Reluctantly, she agreed to share the results of the business with her management team. Their response shocked her. When the management team saw the actual numbers, they were concerned for her! They had assumed the business was much more profitable, the owner was comfortable, her retirement was secure, and she had no reason for concern. Nothing could have been further from the truth. The business was much less profitable than they had assumed. In fact, the cash flow barely serviced the debt and allowed for little reinvestment. The owners had taken very little out of the business, and the owner's retirement was very much at risk. The real facts galvanized the workers in a way other efforts had not. Out of loyalty to the owner, they vowed to improve the business and to eliminate her fears. Being privy to the numbers made the employees feel trusted and fully engaged. The company went on to great success. Some years later, the management team bought the business from the owner, and they continue to run it successfully today.

Double Loop Learning

In order to effectively plan and look beyond the numbers to the system effects, it is critical to use a technique called *double loop learning*. Most managers use a linear problem-solving method, similar to left-brain, action-oriented management and described as *single loop learning* by Chris Argyris.[99] When using this method, you seek out problems directly, and you solve them. That is what we managers do; we handle these situations. During the planning process you need to avoid the temptation to use linear thinking and problem-solving techniques.

As you have no doubt experienced, the enterprise does not always react as expected or as desired. This is because the enterprise is a complex system of systems, which does not respond in a linear fashion. Often the behavior we are seeing is driven by one of our hidden assumptions, and all we are seeing is the result. Argyris suggests that you must employ a deeper more nuanced learning method. He offers double loop learning, which proposes that you must go back and surface the underlying assumptions, goals, values, and mental models that led to the situation in the first place (see Figure 45). He suggests that these powerful forces are usually hidden and assumed long before the situation or result presents

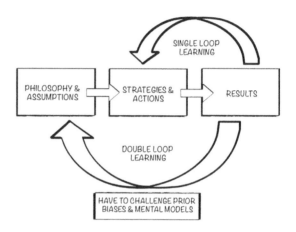

Figure 45. Single and Double Loop Learning

itself. Viewed through the lens of Drucker's *Theory of the Business*[100] this dynamic is clearly revealed—your assumptions underlie everything you do.

As Argyris points out, to move forward you must get past the defensive reasoning. "We have always done it this way" or "Granddad started the business here so we must keep it" are examples of defensive reasoning, which reflects existing assumptions, biases, mental models, or beliefs. Mary Douglas offers a similar caution: "The individual tends to leave the important decisions to his institutions while busying himself with tactics and details."[101]

Going back to our Note from the Field in Chapter 3, the family in question did not get past the defense reasoning and to the underlying assumption, which kept them in the underperforming business. Like most managers, they dutifully kept trying to manage the single loop cycle by refining strategies and trying to improve results.

Do not assume that the simple results you are seeing are indicative. Go beyond the simple and examine the complexity that may have driven the result. Instead of simply seeking out problems and solving them, ask yourself, "Is there a more fundamental, *systemic* reason for the result?" To examine your enterprise in this way it is critical for you to practice the form of mental detachment shown in Figure 44. There is a tendency to view our enterprise from within and through all of the filters and lenses that you have previously put in place, often unconsciously.

Drive the Plan Decisions Down through the Organization

Life is complex in its expression, involving more than percipience, namely desire, emotion, will, and feeling.
—Alfred North Whitehead[102]

After you have a clear plan, you begin the activity of aligning the internal response, the total enterprise system, with the delivery of the satisfiers dictated by the market. Implicit in this charge is assuring that all people in the system see and understand the plan and all its elements clearly enough to complete the hermeneutic story correctly and not make it up. If you do not make the plan and reasons for change visible, the system will tend to ossify around a static view of the market, devolving into stasis, and it will be hard to change as required.

Once you have refined or confirmed the enterprise purpose and have a compelling vision and a plan, cascading the elements of the plan down through the organization, and so building a rich engaging purpose, begins at the boundaries of the area of freedom. These are the inputs to the discussions surrounding the area of freedom.

Picking Up Planning at the Boundaries of the Area of Freedom

The process of proscribing an area of freedom as described in Chapter 9 is used to clarify and rectify assumptions, beliefs, and expectations. There are many good methodologies available, but one in particular that I will call to your attention is Google's OKR process.[103] OKR stands for *objectives* and *key results*. Google uses OKRs to cascade purpose and resulting objectives through the enterprise. The process involves cascading discussions from the CEO down through the enterprise.

First, the plan and objectives are clarified at the enterprise level. Once this is done, key results are developed that must be achieved if the objectives are to be met. These key result areas are developed *with* the individuals and teams who are charged with achieving them. These interactions are repeated down through the entire enterprise to ensure all employees have a clear view of all the objectives and key results at all levels, building the rich engaging purpose described by Bartlett and Ghoshal. Wheatley points out the power of these interchanges:

People who are deeply connected to a cause don't need directives, rewards, or leaders to tell them what to do. Inflamed, passionate, and working with like-minded others, they create increasingly extreme means to support their cause.[104]

The OKR discussions described above cascade assumptions, beliefs, purpose, and commitment down through the enterprise aligning hearts and minds. From these discussions the remainder of the area of freedom conversations are derived, completing the decision phase of the OODA loop and aligning all of the energy fields in the enterprise. All that is left is to act according to the vision, mission, values, and plan of the Enterprise Management System.

Note from the Field

Many of the enterprises I work with are using personas of customers and storyboards of product and service to connect employees to customers and build the rich, engaging purpose. These techniques move away from static descriptions of service or products towards avatars of customers and three-dimensional stories, going beyond the numbers to connect employees to the purpose of the enterprise. Having a customer persona in mind for employees to connect products and services to provides a rich mental model. Additionally, simulations, augmented reality, and gamefied environments can help build understanding and commitment in employees. For example, many companies use multiperiod, financial simulations of companies to teach connectedness for all employees and ingrain concepts of financial performance for nonfinancial employees.

Here are some things you can do, and questions you should ask, to explore and improve the strategic-planning holon in your system:

1. Is your enterprise relentlessly curious about the environment it resides in?
2. Do you have a planning process to capture and harness that curiosity? Is the process tailored to your enterprise? Are your people trained in it, and have they developed the capacity to contribute to it? Do you have planning time built into your yearly schedule?
3. Do your employees know how to engage with the plan? What their roles are?
4. Is the plan visible and known to all? Do you have a process to cascade key system inputs down through the enterprise?
5. Do you have plan reviews built into your schedule (more about this in Chapter 12, "Control and Feedback in the System")?

Key Takeaways
- ✓ Planning is one of the archetypal system holons. You will have a planning process by default or design.
- ✓ Absent a designed planning process, the occupants of the system will derive a plan; they will complete the hermeneutic circle and deduce one.
- ✓ You must have a process to cascade purpose and system inputs down through all of the holons of the enterprise. Absent this, employees will complete their holon inputs themselves.
- ✓ Do not reinvent the wheel. There are great resources for effective planning available to you. What is usually lacking is an enterprise systems-thinking foundation.

Recommended Reading for Chapter 10

Drucker, Peter F. "The Theory of the Business." Harvard Business Review. September–October, 1994.

Bartlett, Christopher A., and Sumantra Ghoshal. "Beyond Strategy to Purpose." Harvard Business Review. November–December, 1994. An insightful look beyond the process of planning to building shared vision, knowledge, and commitment.

Hamel, Gary, and C. K. Prahalad. Competing for the Future. Boston: Harvard Business School Press, 1994. Hamel and Prahalad provide a penetrating look into the need to critically assess the external environment and the factors shaping the business over the long run.

Kim, W. Chan, and Renee Mauborgne. Blue Ocean Strategy. Boston: Harvard Business School Press, 2005. Kim and Mauborgne clearly outline the need to change your viewpoint and perspective in the planning process.

Porter, Michael E. Competitive Advantage: Creating and Sustaining Superior Performance. New York: Simon & Schuster, 1985. Porter is rightfully considered one of the giants of strategic planning.

Christensen, Clayton M. The Innovator's Dilemma. Boston: Harvard Business School Press, 1997. Christensen highlights the stasis that is so dangerous for enterprises and shares methods to combat it.

Aulet, Bill. Disciplined Entrepreneurship: 24 Steps to a Successful Startup. Hoboken: John Wiley & Sons, 2013. Aulet's book is a must read for start-ups and entrepreneurs, but the discipline of planning for markets and product/service offerings is universal and should be utilized by more management teams.

Chapter 11

Structure in the System

One picture is worth ten thousand words.
—Chinese proverb

S tructure is also an *elemental*, dynamic part of the system. Once established, the structure will begin to dictate system behavior in subtle, but provocative, ways. Employees will begin to behave according to their understanding of the structure. Yet, structure is an area where we get complexity and simplicity mixed up in our enterprises. We take a complex structure and render it using only one view. To most employees an enterprise is an incredibly complex entity, yet we typically describe it with just one mental model—the organizational chart. Why constrain ourselves to such a limited, albeit powerful, view?

Note from the Field

Years ago, I asked an architect who was designing a house how many sheets or views were required for the job, and his reply imparted great wisdom about structure. He said, "As many as it takes for the client to see the house in their mind's eye, and the builder to understand how to build it, and the zoning officials to know what they need to approve it."

140

For you and your employees to have a systematic, shared mental model of the structure of your organization, you have to do three things:

1. Share common models of the system structure for all to see.
2. Design and describe the job as a part of the system.
3. Change the structure in response to the market needs and shifts, if necessary.

Models of Your System

Let us learn from architecture and architects. Use as many views as you need to describe your enterprise and assure that your employees understand and recognize the power and peril inherent in the structure.

In the preceding chapters, we have seen several mental models that help us grasp the system. We have seen the *holarchic* view, a hierarchy of holons, which depicts the systemic nature of the enterprise and highlights the critical nature of interactions and the cascading of purpose down through the organization. We have seen the *servant leader model*, which depicts the natural tendency of systems to build from the bottom up and how the higher tiers serve to integrate and coordinate the lower tiers. If these models explain your system, share them. If not, modify them so they accurately reflect your mental model of your system and then, share those. Let us now look at a few more views that are critical to understanding the system.

✓ **The traditional organizational chart.** This view of the system has endured for so long precisely because it is so powerful and revealing. As a map of the structure, it clearly shows where the power and authority to delegate reside. It is a clarifying tool for channels of communication and direction. Do not abandon this traditional tool. Augment it with more views of the system.

✓ **Cross-functional teams.** Most enterprises have multiple cross-functional teams—product development, technology, and customer service teams, for example. We know that a team is a subsystem, a holon, within the greater whole. Map out all of the teams and assure everyone in the system knows the purpose, elements, and interactions of each. These cross-functional views are often similar in nature to the next view.

✓ **Process or horizontal views.** The enterprise is an assemblage of processes. Make sure all employees know the key processes within the system. Figure 46 gives a simple example of such a view.

✓ **Handy's Shamrock.** Charles Handy suggests yet another view of the enterprise with his Shamrock model of the organization.[105] In this view

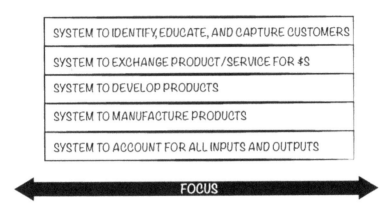

SYSTEM TO IDENTIFY, EDUCATE, AND CAPTURE CUSTOMERS

SYSTEM TO EXCHANGE PRODUCT/SERVICE FOR $S

SYSTEM TO DEVELOP PRODUCTS

SYSTEM TO MANUFACTURE PRODUCTS

SYSTEM TO ACCOUNT FOR ALL INPUTS AND OUTPUTS

FOCUS

Figure 46. Example of High-Level Process View

(shown in Figure 47) the extended, and often critical to success, resources are included in the enterprise view.

Ensuring everyone in the enterprise has common and sufficient views of the system facilitates the needed system exchanges of energy and information. These exchanges of information and energy enable coordination and communication among the holons and promote decentralized decision making directed by a shared purpose and values, assuring alignment.

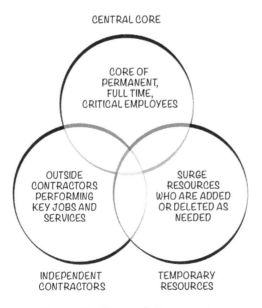

CENTRAL CORE

CORE OF PERMANENT, FULL TIME, CRITICAL EMPLOYEES

OUTSIDE CONTRACTORS PERFORMING KEY JOBS AND SERVICES

SURGE RESOURCES WHO ARE ADDED OR DELETED AS NEEDED

INDEPENDENT CONTRACTORS

TEMPORARY RESOURCES

Figure 47. Shamrock Organization

Fit the Job to the System

The next step in designing your enterprise system structure is to ensure each individual job conforms to the system. Now that you know systems, you should know that you must keep your structures facile, dynamic, and fluid. This is not easy, requiring you to practice another series of *both/and* simplexity gyrations. Your structures must

✓   *both* clearly outline roles *and* promote individual freedom.
✓   be *both* fixed for a certain time to ensure execution of the plan *and* be responsive to changes.
✓   *both* incorporate all of the necessary functions, having sufficient specialization, *and* eliminate bounded rationality.
✓   promote *both* effective spans of control *and* sufficient decentralization.

Individually, these goals are simple and straightforward. Collectively they take on a feeling of complexity. Once again, seek the simple model, adopt it for your enterprise, and then replicate that model through your system. Figure 48 represents a checklist you can use to design your jobs.

Often when owners and managers first see the checklist they remark, "But you told us people are our most important asset, why aren't people at the top of the list?" Here is why. Remember, in the system, there can be no stand-alone jobs. All jobs relate directly to the system. Therefore, you must start the design with the system. Let me explain.

1. *Strategy.* As we will discuss in the next section, your structure should be a reflection of your strategy.
2. *Functions.* The strategies you employ dictate certain functions that must be performed and where they are to be performed.
3. *Processes.* To accomplish the function requires consistent, repeatable processes, which may require specialized skills.

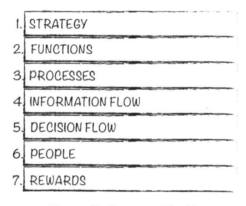

Figure 48. Structure Checklist

4. *Information flow.* The functions also require certain system information flow to the function and through the processes in the function (feedback).
5. *Decision flow.* In sociotechnical systems, you have to contemplate what decisions the individual occupying the job might have to make.
6. *People.* It is not until you have designed all of the above elements that you can assign the correct personnel to the task, or recruit for them. This relates back to our area of freedom. Too great an area of freedom without corresponding competency, can lead to mistakes, misunderstanding, and

frustration. Conversely, too small an area of freedom for an accomplished individual will be a waste of talent for the enterprise and feel restrictive to the employee.

7. *Rewards.* Finally, you must carefully consider the rewards. **Beware:** Remember the system tenet of bounded rationality. Once you describe the boundaries and assign an incentive, your employees will begin to behave according to the subsystem you have designed. Make sure the incentives align with both the local goal (purpose) and the greater enterprise goals and purpose.

The Need for Change in Structure

> *Structure follows strategy.*
> —Alfred D. Chandler Jr.[106]

Chandler's admonition has been a part of management lore for decades. It is good advice. It stems from the fundamental dynamic described in the theory of the business. The environment in which the enterprise operates is constantly changing. Therefore, the systems and processes that are fundamental to delivering goods and services to the environment must also be changing if they are to be effective. Hence, structure must follow strategy. However, structure is an area where stasis is particularly acute.

Most owners and management teams do not realize how powerful the structurally induced system forces are. There is a tendency to assume that our existing structure is sufficient and benign. This is not a good assumption.

Note from the Field

Family businesses often struggle with structurally induced system dynamics. In many family businesses, the family unit serves as a proxy for the structural model for the enterprise. This is not usually an optimal solution. I worked with one family business that dramatically changed its strategy and go-to-market systems due to changes in the environment. Yet when the discussion turned to the structural changes needed, as dictated by the change in strategy, the family became resistant. The expectation was that all family members would remain in their respective functions and with their respective levels of authority and responsibility. Consequently, the family forced a structure that was at cross-purposes with the system. Performance and departmental interactions suffered and family tensions became a dominant system dynamic. Financial performance suffered and the resulting family strife dramatically reduced the value of the business.

Now that you are a systems thinker and know how powerfully structure drives behavior in the system, I hope you will reconsider structure and include a review of it in your management processes. Mary Douglas offers a proper caution in this area:

The instituted community blocks personal curiosity, organizes public memory, and heroically imposes certainty on uncertainty. In marking its own boundaries, it affects all lower-level thinking, so that persons realize their own identities and classify each other through community affiliation. Since it uses a division of labor as a source of metaphors to affirm itself, the community's self-knowledge and knowledge of the world must undergo change when the organization of work changes.[107]

Note from the Field

I know of several companies, which effectively tear up their organizational chart every year after completing the strategic planning process. Their management teams construct a new "should be" structure without names or specific individuals in mind and then conduct a gap analysis with the "as is" structure. Then employees essentially reapply for either their old position or new ones dictated by the strategy. This process drives home the need for all employees to stay current with their jobs or develop in concert with the company direction and strategy.

You may not want to go that far, but I encourage you to take more than a cursory look at your organizational structure. There is a lot more going on with it than you think. It is *both* simple *and* complex.

Here are some things you can do, and questions you should ask, to explore and improve the organizational structure holon in your system:

1. Acknowledge structure as a powerful system component.
2. Ask yourself, "What would my organizational structure look like if I started from scratch?"
3. Draw up your structure on a clean sheet of paper.
4. Perform a gap analysis and ask yourself, "Would I reappoint my current employees to the new positions?"

Key Takeaways

✓ You must provide sufficient views of your system for all occupants to see both the hard system and the soft system aspects of the structure.

✓ Structure is a deceptively powerful system holon, which implies durability, stability, and permanence. Yet, these qualities are only valuable if the structure is also flexible.

✓ Structure follows strategy, and you must review it as your plan changes.

Recommended Reading for Chapter 11

Drucker, Peter F. *The Essential Drucker*. New York: Harper, 2001.
Morgan, Gareth. *Images of Organizations*. Thousand Oaks: Sage Publications, 1997. Morgan's classic offers great insight into the power and complexity of what appears to be a simple construct.
Welch, Jack. *Winning*. New York: Harper Collins, 2005.

Chapter 12

Control and Feedback
in the System

Even though worker capacity and motivation are destroyed when leaders choose power over productivity, it appears that bosses would rather be in control than have the organization work well.
—Margaret Wheatley[108]

C ontrol is a very provocative word. We do not want to be controlled, but we want to be in control. Here is a key systems-thinking insight you have to become comfortable with: the only way you are really in control is if the *system* is in control, and every holon and employee is doing what they should do. Remember, Deming found that the majority of faults, defects, and mistakes are systemic. If you have chosen well, your employees want to do the right thing. Our systems cause them to stray. If you have properly designed your Enterprise Management System, hired well, trained your employees in your systems, and delegated clearly, you can trust your employees to execute. Chisholm and Brown sum up this concept well:

The effectiveness of any organization is an accumulation of those expensive things called brains.[109]

Sounds like Enterprise Model #3 from Chapter 5, The System at Work:

$$\text{RESULTS} = \sum_{N=1}^{\infty} \text{INDIVIDUAL EFFORTS}$$

So how do you know if the system is in control? As a systems thinker, you now know the most important things to be controlled are the purpose, elements, and interactions of the system. These components are shaped by the seven archetypal holons of your Enterprise Management System. Attend to these and control becomes a more holistic and liberating term for everyone in the system.

Again, we come right back to the basic models of the system from Chapter 5 (see Figure 49).

$$E_{IN} = E_{OUT} - \text{LOSSES} \qquad \text{RESULTS} \int [P \times Ss \times Sh \times Ca \times Co]\, L$$

Figure 49. Enterprise Models #2 and #3

The greatest levers you have for control are

- the quality of your plan.
- the quality of your Enterprise Management System.
- the capability and commitment of your employees, both of which are functions of your Enterprise Management System.

Traditional Control Methods

So what are we to do with our traditional methods of control: our financial statements, control charts, sales reports, and others? These are all important, even critical, and you must continue to use them. However, now that you know the danger of *bounded rationality* and point optimization in a system, you should realize many of these control methods are measuring only a part of the whole. Doing this often leads to the temptation to make each part as efficient as possible. Remember the system tenet of *throughput* and the *theory of constraints*. Do not confuse efficiency with effectiveness. It is possible to be efficient at doing the wrong things. Make sure you always consider system effectiveness when optimizing, and assure your control methods reflect the same thinking.

You must also realize your traditional reports represent the *output* of the various subsystems and the whole system, and those results may be *delayed* by days, months, years, and, as we have seen in our examples, even decades. For example, if you have a five-year lease and you are in year four, the lease payments made in the current year are the result of a decision made four years before and that long ago decision affects results today. As you can see in Figure 50, results are a following effect of all of the strategic and tactical decisions the system and its occupants have made over years.

What you see from Figure 50 is a time-delayed graphic view of Enterprise Model #2. Your plan sets into motion the system, which acts on the plan, and the results follow. The system's purpose is made manifest in a series of plans over time. Therefore, progress against the planned objectives becomes the best control means. If you wait until you see the results, it is too late for you to change the result, to manage the outcome. You can only influence future results. Ostensibly, your plan was a future *preferred* state, so tracking progress against plans throughout the system becomes imperative.

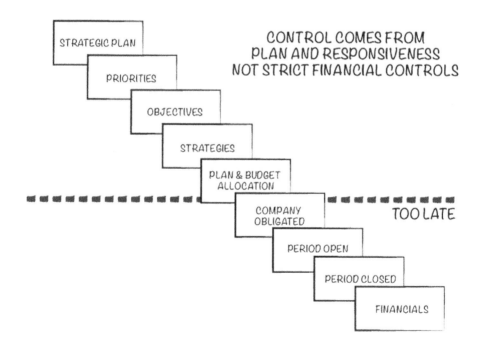

Figure 50. Results, Delays, and Control

Viewed from this perspective, it is clear what needs to be reviewed are the dynamics and decisions that are manifest in the enterprise system holarchy. So what system artifacts reflect these dynamics and decisions? Here is a good starting list, derived directly from basic model #2:

- *Strategic plan reviews.* During the planning process, you determined you needed to do certain things and you developed a series of integrated, nested plans. If progress is important to you, you should ask how you are progressing. Elements include
  - ° total plan reviews.
  - ° action plan reviews.
  - ° departmental plan reviews.
  - ° cross-functional team reviews.
- *Individual performance reviews* (capabilities and competencies). In cascading the plan down through the organization, you assigned certain roles and tasks to employees. How are they doing? Elements include
  - ° individual action or personal performance plan reviews.
  - ° development plan reviews.
  - ° areas of freedom discussions.
- *System reviews.* You have an Enterprise Management System. How is it performing? Review elements include
  - ° leadership reviews to ask how leadership is performing.
  - ° culture reviews to ask if the culture reflects the correct values.
  - ° process and subsystem reviews.
  - ° external verification, or benchmarking against best-in-class competition.

You should conduct your reviews regularly throughout the year. Most successful enterprises schedule them in advance to ensure that all system occupants are aware of the timing. The following are key questions to ask during these reviews:

- Has anything in the external environment changed that would indicate a change in our current plan?
- What is working as planned? Should we do more in areas of progress or success?
- What is not working according to our plan? Is it a result of our performance or an externality? What are we going to do to change or recover?

Some of the classic management books in the recommended reading sections offer great advice on how to plan, execute, and accomplish these reviews.

Note from the Field

Most of the great companies I have seen and worked with do not spend much time on things that are going according to plan, except to praise as needed. If you have been clear in delegation and you trust the employee, you can assume everything is going as planned or the employee would have told you. I recommend you use a stoplight metaphor for plan reviews. If the task is colored green, there is no need to talk about it. If it is colored yellow, it means the reporting party has concerns that the outcome or deliverable is at risk, but the risk is currently only to the task in question. While the risk may be contained, any yellow tasks should prompt a review of dependent tasks in other areas. If the task is colored red, it means you are in recovery mode on this item and you should check system linkages for the potential of other plan tasks to be at risk. Remember, in the system, everything is connected.

A Note on Individual Performance Reviews

Performance reviews are one of the most dreaded tasks in business today. I believe there is a simple explanation for this dread. As a manager, if you have not planned for what the future preferred state of the enterprise looks like (as discussed in Chapter 10) and if you have not then had a frank discussion about the area of freedom in which each employee operates (as discussed in Chapter 9), reviews have no contextual basis. They become popularity discussions, based on perceptions, feelings, and the most recent performance. There is a better way. Figure 51 outlines the key change in the dynamic brought about by conducting the area of freedom discussion in advance. I call this success planning. If in advance, you and your direct report have discussed together what constitutes success, then reviewing becomes much more objective and much less stressful. In fact, you will probably

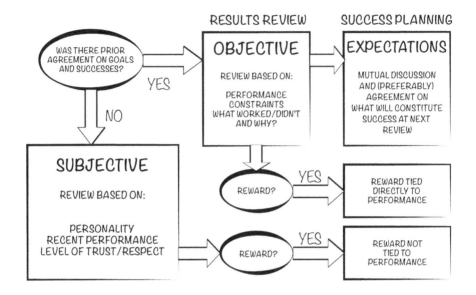

Figure 51. Success Planning and Results Reviews

have reviews many times through the course of the period in question. If you do not have these discussions in advance, the review is subjective and may devolve into being highly emotional.

In conclusion, your Enterprise Management System controls results, not you or any one part of the system. You must design and optimize your Enterprise Management System. Reviewing this construct and keeping it in control will assure that results are in control. Note: This will not make your decisions easier, nor will it ensure success. However, like the executive director in the Preface, you will feel empowered to manage with renewed confidence and skill.

Beware: As a leader in the system, the harder you personally try to control everything, the harder it is to do so. You will set up a rigid system, based on controlling behaviors. This is a static equilibrium and often feels like a psychic prison.

Behold: By designing a sensing and learning Enterprise Management System, you can create a system poised in a dynamic equilibrium, that can respond to change, and one in which the occupants control their own areas of freedom.

Here are some things you can do, and questions you should ask, to explore and improve the control and feedback holon in your system:

1. Develop your Enterprise Management System by design, not by default.
2. Analyze your current systems, processes, control mechanisms, and look for examples of bounded rationality or point optimization. Remember, you optimize the system not necessarily each element.

In Part 3, I will help you begin to design your Enterprise Management System.

Key Takeaways
✓ Control is not rigid adherence to a number or process, it is a fluid concept of tracking activities and progress in the system.
✓ The only way to achieve control is to design your Enterprise Management System.
✓ The tighter you try to control the holons, the more oppressive the system becomes, resulting in reduced throughput.
✓ Sharing information and feedback is critical for system performance and understanding.
✓ Switching to a rhythm of success planning and results reviews changes the individual performance review dynamic.

Recommended Reading for Chapter 12
Goldratt, Eliyahu M. *The Goal: A Process of Ongoing Improvement.* Great Barrington: North River Press, 1984.
Kohn, Alfie. *Punished by Rewards.* New York: Houghton Mifflin, 1993.
Pink, Daniel H. *Drive: The Surprising Truth about What Motivates Us.* New York: Riverhead Books, 2011.
Stack, Jack, and Bo Burlingham. *The Great Game of Business: The Only Sensible Way to Run a Company.* New York: Doubleday, 1992.
Welch, Jack. *Winning.* New York: Harper Collins, 2005.

Part 3

Designing Your Enterprise
Management System

Chapter 13

Orientation and Diagnosis

We learn to do neither by thinking nor by doing. We learn to do by thinking about what we are doing.
—George Stoddard[110]

Often as managers, we just start doing things. We are action oriented and we are expected to act and direct. Hired into an existing system, we begin to manage according to our experience. As systems thinkers, trained to use Boyd's OODA loop, I hope you now realize the danger inherent in just *doing*. The first step is observing the current system and becoming oriented to it.

Note from the Field

I worked with a large manufacturer that was scaling up for growth. The company hired very experienced senior managers from some of the leading companies you read about in the news. Trained in the "corporate universities" of their prior companies, these individuals had received some of the best management training available. You would think that this "A" team would be excellent at executing, but they struggled. Each was highly competent, but they brought with them the previous *management models on which they had been trained. They had embedded mental models of the way they managed at the old company. In some cases, their prior experience was invaluable. However, in other cases competing management models and language from each of the prior companies caused confusion, resentment, and disorientation. There were examples of the same graphic being used for different purposes and with different language in different departments. Until the new team members harmonized and adapted all the processes, mental models, and language for the current system, they underperformed.*

As Mary Douglas warned in *How Institutions Think*, you must be aware of how powerful the grip of the institution, the system, is on your thoughts and actions and those of the other current occupants.

The place to start in diagnosing your current enterprise is with observing the current state of the common holons.

Diagnosing Your Current System

Remember from Chapter 1 that your current enterprise is already a functioning system, which contains the seven holons of an archetypal system. You can use this model, shown again in Figure 52, as a diagnostic tool to gauge the health of your current enterprise system.

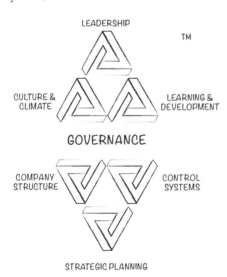

Based on the information you learned from the chapters on the individual holons, how would you rate your enterprise with respect to the archetype? Do you, your management team, and your employees have clear, shared mental models and language for each holon? Are the processes and control methods systemic or local? Are they sufficient? Have you trained everyone in your system?

Figure 52. The Archetype

Helpful hint: Visit http://simplecomplexitybook.com/ to download a free assessment tool to diagnose your current enterprise system. Simply answer a few questions concerning each holon and you will have a baseline score for each one.

After you have assessed each holon and the system as a whole, you will probably have areas of weakness; gaps where you perceive your system is not designed properly. Prioritize your list of holons to work on, and using the preceding chapters and recommended readings, begin to design the Enterprise Management System that is right for you and your enterprise. If models, tools, techniques from *Simple_Complexity* or the recommended readings or friends work as is, use them. If not, modify them to fit *your* EMS.

Beware: As we will discuss in the next chapter, "Change and the System," your findings will most likely lead to new behaviors, models, structures, language. Do not visit all of these changes on your employees all at once. Your people will need to absorb the same information you have and either reconstruct their current, or develop new, schemata. They have to learn the new, system-thinking ways.

Behold: If you include your employees in designing the system, you can unlock an extraordinary level of knowledge, energy, and passion and make it available to the system, your enterprise.

Since you are probably running or managing an existing enterprise, you cannot stop everything while you retool your EMS. Fortunately, I have found that most companies are not profoundly broken. They are usually misaligned in many of the ways we have discussed in the prior chapters.

Diagnosing Your Current Occupants

We expected that good-to-great leaders would begin by setting a new vision and strategy. We found instead that they first got the right people on the bus, the wrong people off the bus, and the right people in the right seats.
—Jim Collins[111]

Once you have a clear understanding of what your Enterprise Management System *should* look like, you will need to assess the current occupants in light of the new model, and conduct a gap analysis similar to the one you performed with the holons. Jim Collins's finding and admonition above is significant at this point. It is far easier to construct your new EMS and achieve a compelling purpose and goals with the right people in your system and in the right roles, and the wrong people out of the system.

To conduct this assessment, you can use your current organizational chart, but instead of just a name in each position, add the construct shown in Figure 53.

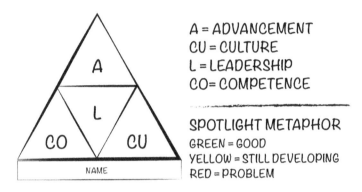

Figure 53. Organizational Assessment Tool

Using the altered organization chart shown above and a stoplight metaphor, map out your entire organization and rate each member of your enterprise as to the following:

- Their fit with the cultural norms you have established (Cu)
- Their leadership qualities and fit with expected norms (L)
- Their competency to fulfill the role they are playing today (Co)
- The potential to advance them in your holarchy (A)

The resulting map of your current organization will graphically reveal key areas where you will need to intervene in the system to provide guidance, development, mentoring; where you may want to move certain people to different roles; and those instances where maybe you should part ways with an individual who really does not fit your system.

Beware: Do not use this methodology or document cavalierly, and of course, do not post it for all to see. It is a powerful tool used well, but you must use it judiciously.

Behold: Leaders at every level of the holarchy using this technique throughout your enterprise can reveal powerful insights into the system and system behavior. The assessments and findings can, and should be, used in conjunction with your learning and development systems and area of freedom discussions.

Setting Up Your Own Corporate University

In the process of diagnosing and designing your EMS, effectively you will be developing the content for your corporate university. Keep good records of all your findings and agreed upon system elements. Summarize and convert them to training and development tools—presentation slides, employee handbook, videos, etc. Start a lending library of the management books that best illustrated certain topics to you. Most importantly, start training everyone in the system to begin developing their capabilities and competencies.

What to Do with What You Find

Using the above diagnostic methods, you will undoubtedly find many things about your current system you will want to change. The next chapter, "Change and the System," will help you plan and execute the desired changes.

Key Takeaways

- ✓ Prospectively design your future Enterprise Management System.
- ✓ Conduct "as is" to "should be" diagnosis.
- ✓ Identify key changes.
- ✓ Prioritize the changes and begin to bring your system into line with your new EMS model.

Chapter 14

Change and the System

The talk you hear about adapting to change is not only stupid, it's dangerous.
The only way you can manage change is to create it. By the time you catch up
to change, the competition is ahead of you.
—Peter Drucker[112]

D rucker's quote, and hopefully this book, will provoke you to view change as an imperative. You know Drucker is correct, because you know your environment is always changing. Additionally, if you have conducted the diagnostics from Chapter 13, you no doubt have some changes you would like to make to your system. However, now that you have a systems perspective, you can see why change is so hard. Your system takes on a life of its own as a complex web of interactions, beliefs, assumptions, mental models, and processes. Undoing and redoing this web is hard and takes time.

It takes time to design and build an enterprise that is poised on the knife-edge of dynamic equilibrium to be ready for the required change. If you do not have such an enterprise, chances are your organization is experiencing some sort of stasis and will be resistant to change. The amount of resistance is determined by the following factors:

1. *The extent of the stasis.* Progress towards your new, future preferred state will depend on how entrenched the current stasis is, how wrenching the contemplated change is, what is at stake in the changes, and how well you prepare your employees for the journey.

162

2. *The size of the enterprise.* It is far easier to change a small, close-knit company, than a large sprawling enterprise.
3. *The extent and rate of change.* How fast and far the current system and its occupants have to travel.

As you can see in Figure 54, there is an inverse relationship between the average experience each member of your enterprise has with the new reality and the rate of change. The gap you see is the reorientation and development gap you must overcome to get to a new state of dynamic equilibrium. Fortunately, if the rate of change is low, the need for dramatic reorientation and development is also low. Unfortunately, if the rate of change is aggressive, the gap widens quickly.

The greater the rate of change, the greater will be the need for changing the hearts, minds, mental models, and language within the holons of the system. The greater the change is, the greater the need for reorientation.

Change brings with it great uncertainty unless we are very clear and very precise with our expectations and language. Change means leaving behind one environment—with its attendant routines, processes,

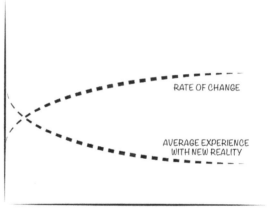

Figure 54. Development Gap

mental models, language, and rewards, both intrinsic and extrinsic—and embracing another. The time between the start of the change process and the time when we are comfortable with the new reality is a time of ambiguity and uncertainty with the new environment. Your employees will feel confused and in many cases resentful. Employees will be torn, between allegiance to the old, comfortable way, which you told them was expected, and the new, uncomfortable way, which is foreign, but now expected. Left alone with these feelings, an employee may feel uninvolved, uninformed, and abandoned. Put simply, change puts stress on the organization.

Stress and the Organization

There are various models of stress used to show the phases an individual may traverse when under stress. Figure 55 highlights one such model. Faced with ambiguous situations employees may feel caught in a state of uncertainty. If they reside in this state for too long, the feelings of uncertainty can lead to feelings of a loss of control. These feelings of a loss of control often manifest themselves as stress. Left unchecked these feelings of stress can result in detrimental behaviors.

As we know, the system is an assemblage of its people. Therefore, organizations are subject to the same risks. We also know that enterprises face ambiguous situations as a normal course of business. We deal with these by developing assumptions about the situation, thereby rendering us *certain* of our response. Assumptions act as a filter of certainty for the organization, eliminating uncertainty and restoring a feeling of control (see Figure 56). This is precisely why management must share its assumptions with the rest of the occupants of the system. Absent this filter, uncertainty, loss of control, and stress can cascade down through the enterprise. Individuals will develop their own assumptions about the new reality. They will traverse the hermeneutic circle and complete the story. Some will see the gaps between the reality and the system's response and be fearful. Some will be angry, and some will be confused.

Wheatley clearly articulates this dynamic:

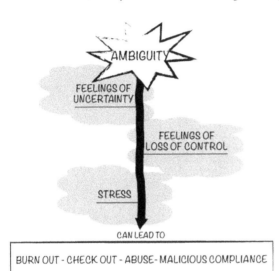

Figure 55. Phases of Stress

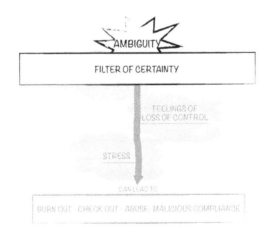

Figure 56. Management Provides a Filter of Certainty

But there is a way out of the paralyzing fear that ambiguity engenders. It requires that we step back, refocus our attention on the system as a whole, and realize there are other processes at work. Beyond our leadership skills, and often in spite of them, the system is self-organizing.[113]

Your job as a leader and manager is to insert a filter of certainty in times of ambiguity, in times of change. The way to do this is to reveal the realities requiring the change and reorient every holon in the system to the new reality. This can only occur through the types of conversations we discussed in the previous chapters. You must rebuild the rich engaging *purpose*, retool the *interactions*, and redevelop the *elements* of your system in light of the new realities.

The Change Continuum

There are many very useful models for organizational change. All of them attempt to explain the complex dynamics affecting people experiencing change. Most change specialists use the analogy that employees grieve the loss of the known as much as or more than, they fear the change. This is a rational systemic response. They are comfortable with the system, as it is currently constructed, or as you have defined it for them, and they will grieve and fear the loss of this comfort. They can be said to *believe* in the current system and we know from Peirce's work that people become fixated on their beliefs and resist changing them. The Kübler-Ross Grief Cycle is particularly revealing.[114] In it there are five stages of the cycle, all with different attendant responses:

- *Anger.* Employees are often angry about the changes. This anger can spring from many sources—not being included in planning the proposed changes, loss of value through the proposed change, etc.
- *Bargaining.* Employees will often first begin to bargain to maintain the status quo or delay the change. Managers often resent this, but it can actually be a sign of respect for the old ways.
- *Depression.* Once it is inevitable that the change will occur, employees often become depressed or despondent.
- *Acceptance.* After some period, employees will come to accept the change. Note: acceptance does not necessarily mean agreement. It only means the change has been assimilated into the new normal. However, that new normal may be unsettled.

Viewed graphically, the cycle looks like Figure 57.

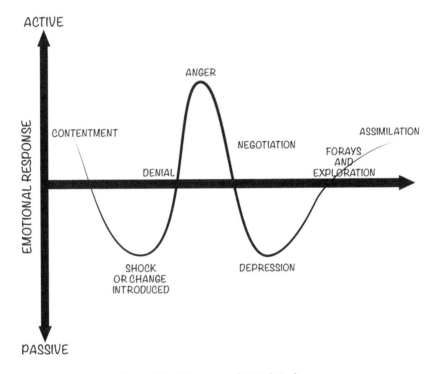

Figure 57. Change and Grief Cycle

As you will note from this model, the person experiencing the change goes through different phases and experiences, different feelings, exhibits different needs, and needs different supervision and management. The denial phase is particularly disruptive. Depending on the extent of the change, the individual may have lost all past mental models and comfortable routines. Employees may feel ignorant, fearful, resentful, but because of business decorum, may not exhibit any outward signs. This is where the sensing component of thought leadership is so important. You should also note that if the change or shock is minimal there might be little to no visible signs of duress. Additionally, note that acceptance does not necessarily mean agreement. It may only mean that the individual has accepted the change and become accustomed to the new environment. However, there may still be resentment or bitterness, leading to malicious compliance. As leaders, we must help guide our employees through these phases by listening and sensing for signs of duress.

The reader should take careful note of the initial phases of both the change/ grief cycle and the knowledge continuum discussed earlier. The early phase of each involves confusion, ambiguity, and stress. It is not comfortable to be "consciously incompetent" as depicted in Figure 38 in Chapter 9. If the employees experiencing these feelings do not have belief in the need to change and a clear mental model of what to change to, they will experience cognitive dissonance.

Cognitive Dissonance

Cognitive dissonance, a theory popularized by Leon Festinger, is an uncomfortable feeling caused by holding conflicting ideas simultaneously. The theory of cognitive dissonance proposes that people have a motivational drive to reduce dissonance and gain internal consistency. They do this by changing their attitudes, beliefs, and actions.[115] Employees also attempt to reduce cognitive dissonance by justifying, blaming, and denying the change or the change agent. Remember that Peirce suggests in *The Fixation of Beliefs* that we are most uncomfortable when we are so disquieted. However, this is precisely when we are open to changing our beliefs.[116] Therefore, it is an inevitable waypoint along the journey of the continuum. What is important for leaders and managers in the system is to realize that cognitive dissonance reduces the area of freedom (see Figure 58).

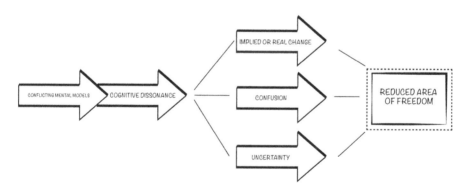

Figure 58. Reduced Area of Freedom

Your employees will retreat to comfortable behaviors and routines, or lash out due to stress or both. Any of these actions reduces effectiveness and reduces both holon and system throughput. It is very helpful to share these mental models with your subordinates and teammates. Knowledge of what they are feeling and why they are feeling it will help them more quickly feel comfortable in the new environment and traverse the continuums faster, thereby reexpanding their areas of freedom. Often just knowing that what they are feeling is normal is comforting and encouraging.

Leadership Style and Change

In times of crisis or rapid change, action leadership and a style preference towards action can actually be counterproductive. Management's typical responses during these times are to push harder, go faster, change procedures rapidly and often, and speak more urgently. The pressure is on, so do something! Based on the change/grief continuum and the knowledge continuum from Chapter 9, these bold actions actually increase the confusion and stress and decrease the speed and effectiveness of progression through both. From a systems perspective they also drive more shock waves through the system increasing the chances of unintended consequences. Counterintuitively, in times of crisis when action seems most appropriate this is precisely when senior leadership needs to utilize thought leadership and examine the system effects. A crisis represents an opportunity to think.

Thought and Emotional Leadership Is the Way Forward

To lead others is to help them change their
thoughts, beliefs, and actions for the better.
—Jim Rohn

It is an old saw now, but change is inevitable. Progressing with that change is a personal option all leaders have to consider for themselves and their staff. During times of extreme change, once governance sets the purpose for the enterprise, leadership should be at the center of the Enterprise Management System because it is the most influential of all the system holons and leaders are the most influential change agents. This dictates that leaders be effective change agents and learn the human dynamics associated with personal and organizational change. Note that this centrality of leadership implies leaders also have the potential to be the biggest *obstacles* to change.

What gets people through change is leadership that shows them the future and assures them that the leaders will safely help them navigate to it. You have to reach everyone. People need leadership in these times. You cannot berate people to new understandings or to greatness. You have to inspire them. You have to be clear about what the change means to them. It is key to remember that people learn using different modalities—auditory, visual (graphical and linear), sensory, etc., and at different rates. Therefore, do not strive to be efficient. Strive to be effective.

Leadership must remember that individuals coping with change, learning new techniques and concepts, and developing anew need the following:

- ✓ Context for the new learning
- ✓ Clear understanding of new assumptions and mental models
- ✓ Clear, concise, consistent language (to include definitions for new or redefined terms)
- ✓ Repetition
- ✓ Visuals—posted mental models, user guides
- ✓ Time—both team and individual
- ✓ Leadership and mentoring

Finally, some employees may choose not to, or cannot, make the transition to the new reality. Removing these resistors from the system is critical for progress.

The Simplicity and Complexity Inversion

Traversing the knowledge and change/grief continuums we have discussed can cause an inversion in simplicity and complexity. As a manager who has traversed the knowledge continuum towards being expert, you have the benefit of context and a more complete understanding of the new reality and the effect on the system. You have traveled around the hermeneutical circle more times. From your viewpoint, with your experience, the system may now seem simple. You probably have become assimilated to the changes. From your viewpoint, the new reality may seem very simple and nonthreatening. However, your employees are lagging behind on both continuums and the view forward may look complex and daunting.

Beware: Remember the systemicity and Whitehead's caution not to trust the simplicity you see. Remember that your subordinates may not have your experience or context and will be viewing the system from a different viewpoint. Like our listeners in Chapter 2 who could not understand the simple description of doing laundry, what appears simple to you may seem complex and incomprehensible to them.

Behold: Simply providing context and adopting a leadership style of mentoring and guiding can dramatically change the absorption and comprehension of new information and ideas.

Beer, Eisenstat, and Spector in *Why Change Programs Don't Produce Change*[117] summarize the best practice elements for change management:

✓ Mobilize commitment through *joint* diagnosis of problems.
✓ Develop a *shared* vision of how to move forward—new mental models, new roles, and new rewards.
✓ Foster consensus for the new vision, build commitment, cohesion, and new competencies.
✓ Spread new ways organically to revitalize the organization.
✓ Institutionalize the new way through policies, systems, structures, reports, etc.
✓ Monitor compliance and make corrections as needed.
✓ Replace noncompliers.

Key Takeaways

✓ Change is inevitable, yet progress is optional. Embracing the needed change is the choice of leadership.
✓ The enterprise can be built to be better able to adapt to change, but leadership has to build the enterprise that way.
✓ Resistance to change is a backhanded compliment to management and the employees' way of protecting the old system you designed for them. Some will grieve the loss of the old system.
✓ Even experienced people will feel awkward in the new reality; they are back to being a novice in the new order.
✓ If leadership does not help them with the change, people will take it personally and feel alone or unappreciated.
✓ There will be a tendency to revert to the old comfortable ways. People will want more time. Leadership must reflect the changes constantly and reward the new behaviors.

Recommended Reading for Chapter 14

Cotter, John P. *Leading Change.* Boston: Harvard Business School Press, 1996. Cotter's book on organizational change is a classic.

Gardner, Howard. *Changing Minds.* Boston: Harvard Business School Press, 2006.

Goleman, Daniel. *Emotional Intelligence: Why It Can Matter More Than IQ.* New York: Bantam, 1995.

Jick, Todd D. *Managing Change: Cases and Concepts.* Boston: Irwin, 1993. Also a classic with many great case study examples.

Medina, Jon. *Brain Rules*. Seattle: Pear Press, 2014.

Pink, Daniel H. *Drive: The Surprising Truth about What Motivates Us*. New York: Riverhead Books, 2011.

Sinek, Simon. *Start with Why*. New York: Penguin, 2009.

Chapter 15

Processes, Technology, Innovation, and the System

It isn't uncommon for managers at senior levels of large organizations
to be so out of touch with customer or production reality that they
don't know just how broken some of their business processes are.
—Michael Hammer & James Champy[118]

One of my industrial engineering professors, Anko Prak, told our assembled class in the seventies "the enterprise is merely an assemblage of all its processes." He was an engineer and not a systems thinker, so we will forgive him for ignoring the soft system components, but he was correct. Hammer and Champy brought this fact to the masses in their illuminating book, *Reengineering the Corporation.*

Processes and Technology

In addition to the most common holons, your system has an enormous number of processes. In my experience, most managers have not really inventoried and optimized them. Your system, and the people in it charged with converting inputs into outputs, will develop these processes with or without your guidance. Take to heart the admonitions of Hammer, Champy, Dr. Prak, and others. Inventory and optimize your system processes. Engage your employees in this exercise to build the rich engaging purpose described herein. The American Productivity and Quality

Center[119] and others have inventories of general business process models and resources available for download.

Beware: Processes and the introduction of new technology are areas where management often practices bounded rationality. For example, the IT department will introduce a new software tool that helps it manage remote log-on, but also compromises productivity for the field sales force. Processes and technology often have an enterprise-wide impact. However, they are often managed by a department or function below the CEO, and as an unintended result, the enterprise view is lost or compromised. Additionally, many CEOs are not comfortable with or sufficiently aware of the reach of the technical or process changes and often delegate the task without a sufficient appreciation of the systemic impact.[120]

Additionally, you must be very careful to assure alignment of processes when bringing on managers. As we discussed in previous chapters, they may come in with powerful mental models that are not in alignment with your system.

Innovation

Large corporations are often managed using incentives to maximize return on equity derived from the du Pont identity.[121] The du Pont identity breaks return on equity down into terms of sales efficiency, asset efficiency, and financial efficiency. The focus is entirely on efficiency as it should be. However, a focus on return on sales, return on assets, asset turnover, and free cash flow in conjunction with short-term time horizons creates a system that is largely incompatible with creativity and innovation. Creativity and innovation are seldom efficient.

Additionally, the corporate culture must support the often messy, unpredictable nature of creativity and the innovation process. Often in their desire to manage for predictable, repeatable results, corporations *systematize* out creativity, and innovation capabilities.

Note from the Field

I worked with a multinational corporation where managing according to the du Pont identity and short-term financial focus came together to squelch innovation.

By their own admission, leadership said they were bad at innovation, so the CEO was pushing the company to become more innovative, actively promoting innovation at all company events and meetings. In spite of these efforts, innovation remained elusive. I pointed out that their enterprise was perfectly designed to get the results it was getting, which is why they had developed an enterprise that systematically eliminated innovation. Their financial incentives all aligned with the du Pont identity terms of return on sales and return on assets almost assuring that individual managers would not take the necessary steps to spawn innovation. Additionally, the culture was one of a high degree of control and conformity. There was no chance for serendipity and very little room for nonlinear thought. Not surprisingly, the people in the system who were innovative left for better opportunities when possible, and new entrants could sense the rigidity and lack of support for innovation and thus stayed away. In spite of all the training, the enterprise remains stubbornly resistant to the systemic changes necessary to embrace innovation. As is usually the case, merger and acquisition acts as a proxy for innovation by acquiring innovative companies after the marketplace has proven innovation successful. However, the company usually loses the truly innovative people and processes shortly after the acquisition is integrated.

Adding regular process, technology, and innovation reviews to your senior management agenda can help surface some of these issues and assure that critical processes remain effective systemically, not locally. Specifically valuing innovation and creativity and providing the time, space, and incentives for innovation are crucial to the system embracing a culture that supports innovation.

Key Takeaways
✓ Watch for bounded rationality compromising process and technology initiatives.

✓ If the enterprise is deficient in an area, check the system first. It has probably been designed to eliminate or minimize that area.
✓ Competing goals—innovation and return on equity—require balance and *both/and* thinking.

Recommended Reading for Chapter 15

Christensen, Clayton M. *The Innovator's Dilemma*. Boston: Harvard Business School Press, 1997.
Goldratt, Eliyahu M. *The Goal: A Process of Ongoing Improvement*. Great Barrington: North River Press, 1984.
Hammer, Michael, and James Champy. *Reengineering the Corporation*. New York: Harper, 1993.
Heskett, James L., W. Earl Sasser, and Leonard A. Schlesinger. *The Service Profit Chain*. New York: The Free Press, 1997.
Womack, James P., and Daniel T. Jones. *Lean Thinking: Banish Waste and Create Wealth in Your Corporation*. New York: The Free Press, 1996.

Chapter 16

Family Businesses and the System

I can protect myself from my enemies; may God protect me from my family!
—Italian proverb

Success is relative. Become successful and you'll hear from all your relatives!
—Anonymous

The majority of the businesses in the world are small and family businesses. These enterprises affect a vast number of people, and they are systems. Often the family system acts as a proxy for the Enterprise Management System. Families often view them as the same. Sometimes this arrangement works, but it can be perilous, particularly with multigenerational family businesses. A very small percent of family businesses pass from generation to generation. At the time of this writing, according to the Family Firm Institute,[122] approximately 30 percent pass on to the second generation, about 12 percent on to the third generation, and only about 3 percent on to the fourth generation or beyond. Many factors go into these rates, but I believe one is the phenomenon of the family system acting as a proxy for the enterprise system. It is very hard to transfer the value of the family system to another owner.

For the sake of their longevity, family businesses would do well to adopt the practices described in *Simple_Complexity*. The goal is to have an Enterprise Management System that happens to be populated by family members versus a family management system that happens to run the enterprise.

Note from the Field

I worked with a family business in which a mother, father, and four sons held all the top management positions in the business. The enterprise was successful and in a very attractive market. However, the family decided to sell the business instead of transitioning it to the next generation. One of the reasons for this was that the family members could not agree on an equitable way to transition the business. A business broker who happened to be a friend of mine asked me to get involved when no attractive offers were forthcoming. The biggest negative factor was that all of the family members wanted to leave the business upon the sale. The trouble with this approach was that the buyer would now have to provide a brand new management team, and much of the value in the enterprise would walk out the door after the sale. The family members represented key elements and interactions of the system. Therefore, the potential buyers discounted the value of the business. Consequently, the family set about the task of converting the business to a professionally managed enterprise that just happened to have family members performing some of the roles. They had to delegate more and develop their people to make the enterprise more robust, sustainable, and valuable. The transformation took many years and required them to delay their desire of selling the business.

Families at Cross-Purposes

Transferring businesses from generation to generation is hard and emotional. Doing it fairly and smoothly takes time, planning, and communication. Family members being at cross-purposes can often tear apart family businesses. One branch of the family wants to sell the business, for example, while the other wants to keep it. One member works in the business and another does not, but they derive the same benefit from the business, which breeds resentment. Since purpose is fundamental to the system, disagreements in this area are particularly detrimental to the enterprise. Similarly, since the system is always communicating in ways both direct and indirect, disagreements in purpose tend to cascade through the enterprise.

A very useful technique for family businesses so situated is to develop a family business constitution.

The Family Business Constitution

The family business constitution defines the three parts of the system—*purpose*, *elements*, and *interactions*—as they relate to the family.

> **Purpose.** The constitution should define the purpose for the family business or businesses. Is it to provide a lifestyle and jobs to the family, create wealth for family members, provide benefit to the community, or all of the above? Clearly articulating the purpose of the business is critical for all family members to be able to orient themselves to the business and align with that purpose.
>
> **Elements.** The constitution should define how a family member could participate as an active element, a holon, in the business system. What are the expectations for work ethic, pay, training, competency, etc.? Clarity in this area removes much of the emotion from the decision to bring on a family member. Does the family member want to be a part of the business? Does he or she have the required training and experience for the business? How will the family member benefit from being a part of the family business, and how is this different from a nonparticipant's benefits?
>
> **Interactions.** The constitution should define the values, beliefs, assumptions, and expectations that will shape the interactions in the system. Clarity in this area assures that family members behave in ways that are consistent with the system as a whole and not allowed to diverge by virtue of their family ties.

According to Williams and Presser, 60 percent of all family business transitions fail due to problems with communication and trust. Further, 25 percent fail due to a lack of preparation on the part of the next generation.[123] The process of developing and continuing a family business constitution forces the necessary communication and next generation preparation to combat these failure modes.

Note from the Field

I worked with a family business to implement many of the techniques described in this book. The recently named CEO from the fourth generation approached me to help with many business issues. He had become CEO after a rather contentious transition battle, and he suspected that the issues had more to do with family issues than with business issues. This proved to be the case. The business has three distinct businesses and family members from generation three through four were scattered among the businesses and the management teams. Generation five was looming on the horizon. The overall business was very successful and provided a great lifestyle to the extended family. However, the CEO described two problems. He suspected that the businesses were less successful than they could be, and that in spite of the success, family relations were severely strained. We set to work on both problems. We used the methods described in the preceding chapters to address the business issues, and we convened the family to tackle the family issues. We used the development of a family constitution to clarify the three key components of the system. These were not easy discussions, but addressing them outside of the ongoing businesses kept the contention from cascading through the businesses to a large degree. Key outcomes from this exercise fall into three categories:

1. Purpose. The family moved away from a view of the system as a provider of lifestyle to the family members and towards viewing it as an investment portfolio that provided for the families. Boards of directors were established, with outside directors for perspective in governance and deep experience in the defined businesses.

2. *Elements.* The constitution established that all positions in the enterprises be filled with candidates who had the experience, skills, competence, values, and passion required for the position. Family members were encouraged to apply for those positions for which they were qualified. All positions were paid according to market rates. Next generation family members were required to work for a nonrelated business for two years before applying to the family business. A family council was established to arbitrate family issues that arose to keep them out of board meetings and day-to-day operations.

3. *Interactions.* The values of the family were defined and promulgated. Expectations for behaviors and adherence were established. Under the new constitution, family members were held to a higher standard than nonfamily members, reflecting the belief that most employees would believe that family members got their jobs by virtue of their name, not their skills.

These changes took many years and were accompanied by a great deal of frustration, acrimony, and debate. However, the family businesses are now run much more smoothly, and the family issues are dealt with outside of the businesses. All of the businesses are now professionally managed enterprises that are treated as a portfolio of assets and reviewed by the family for appropriate levels of risk and reward.

There is ample information on the development of family constitutions, and many resources available to family businesses. I commend them to you. You do not have to struggle with these issues alone.

Key Takeaways

✓ The family management system can act as the Enterprise Management System, but you must be careful. Much more is at stake than just the business.

✓ Family relationships can be a source of great strength for the enterprise, but they can be equally damaging.

✓ DNA is not a good determinant of competency or desire. Make sure the family member wants to be in the role he or she is in and has the competency to be effective.

Recommended Reading for Chapter 16

The Family Firm Institute, Inc. has many great resources for family businesses including a bookstore dedicated to the topic: http://www.ffi. org/?page=ebookstore.

Chapter 17

Final Thoughts

Everything should be made as simple as possible, but not simpler.
—Albert Einstein

Senge said the fifth discipline is systems thinking because "it is the discipline that integrates the disciplines."[124] I believe it is also the missing ingredient for most leaders, managers, and owners. He wrote, "Perhaps the single greatest liability of management teams is that they confront these complex, dynamic realities [in their enterprises] with a language designed for simple, static problems."[125] You have seen and felt the effects of the system swirling around you. You have intuitively sensed that there is a system at work in your enterprise. What has been missing is a language and set of mental models, a schema that brings it all into focus. I hope that *Simple_Complexity* has helped to bring your enterprise into clearer focus. I hope that what appeared to be a hopelessly complex construct has become simpler and more approachable. I hope you can see that the complexity comes from an enormous number of simple *elements*, which *interact* on *purpose*. I hope you can see the beauty and elegance of the system and sense its immense power. I hope you now **behold** the system in all of its *Simple_Complexity*.

Miles Menander Dawson wrote that the most fundamental advice one could derive from the basic teachings of Confucius was to "cultivate oneself with reverential care."[126] I hope that you will adopt this approach to the development of your Enterprise Management System. If you will attend to the three basic components of your enterprise with reverential care, I believe you will succeed.

✓ Cultivate the *purpose* with reverential care. Make sure you and everyone in the system grasps and connects with the purpose. Make it a worthy purpose that inspires. Use leadership and your planning process to cascade a rich engaging purpose down through your enterprise. Invite people to connect to that purpose and live it.

✓ Choose the *elements* of your system—be they people or teams or processes—with reverential care. Develop your employees' skills, capabilities, and commitment with reverential care and let them do the same for others.

✓ Tend to the *interactions* of your system with reverential care. Life is too short to live in or be warden to a psychic prison. Build a system of shared purpose, vision, values, and commitment. Grant people clear, inspiring areas of freedom where they can grow and prosper.

I wish you good luck and Godspeed. You'd best start believing in systems, you're in one!

Notes

1 Tom Northup, *Five Hidden Mistakes CEOs Make: How to Unlock the Secrets That Drive Growth and Profitability* (Queensland: Solutions Press, 2008).

2 Margaret J. Wheatley, *Leadership and the New Science: Discovering Order in a Chaotic World* (San Francisco: Berrett-Koehler Publishers, 2006), 5.

3 Peter Senge, *The Fifth Discipline* (New York: Doubleday, 1990).

4 Paraphrased from Donella H. Meadows, *Thinking in Systems: A Primer* (White River Junction: Chelsea Green Publishing Company, 2008), 11.

5 Simon Sineck, *Start with Why: How Great Leaders Inspire Everyone to Take Action*, (New York: Penguin, 2009).

6 Ludwig von Bertalanffy, *General Systems Theory* (New York: George Braziller, Inc., 1969).

7 http://www.merriam-webster.com/dictionary/complexify. Webster's defines *complexify* as "to become complex."

8 Morgan coined the metaphor "psychic prison" in 1986 as a way to depict employees becoming trapped within controlling organizations.

9 Donella H. Meadows, *Thinking in Systems: A Primer* (White River Junction: Chelsea Green Publishing Company, 2008), 95.

10 Donella H. Meadows, *Thinking in Systems: A Primer,* (White River Junction: Chelsea Green Publishing Company, 2008), 99.

11   Herbert Simon, "Theories of Bounded Rationality" in R. Radner and C. B. McGuire, eds., *Decisions and Organization* (Amsterdam: North-Holland Publishing Company, 1972).

12   https://en.wikipedia.org/wiki/Hermeneutic_circle.

13   Arthur Koestler, *The Ghost in the Machine* (New York: Penguin, 1967).

14   John R. Boyd is credited with developing the OODA Loop. He never wrote a book about military history or the application of it to business. However, Robert Greene, praised its effectiveness in a post entitled *OODA and You*, and it has become legendary.

15   Jean Piaget, *The Origin of Intelligence in the Child* (New York: Routledge & Kegan Paul, 1953).

16   Peter Senge, *The Fifth Discipline* (New York: Doubleday, 1990), 8.

17   Alan Kay was a researcher at Xerox's famous Palo Alto Research Center (PARC). He is a Fellow of the American Academy of Arts and Sciences, the National Academy of Engineering, and the Royal Society of Arts.

18   Jean Piaget studied cognitive development as a psychologist and proposed the idea of schemas as building blocks of knowledge.

19   Jon Medina, *Brain Rules: Twelve Principles for Surviving and Thriving at Work, Home, and School* (Seattle: Pear Press, 2014).

20   https://www.youtube.com/watch?v=mzbRpMlEHzM.

21   Jeff Hawkins, *On Intelligence* (New York: Times Books, 2004).

22   Thor Heyerdahl, *Fatu-Hiva - Back to Nature* (Garden City, NY: Doubleday & Company, Inc., 1975).

23   Donella H. Meadows, *Thinking in Systems: A Primer* (White River Junction: Chelsea Green Publishing Company, 2008).

24   Russell Ackoff, "The Future of Operational Research Is Past," *Journal of the Operational Research Society* 30, no. 2 (February 1979): 93–104.

25   Herbert Simon, *Models of Man* (New York: Wiley, 1957).

26   Roger L. Martin, *The Opposable Mind: Winning Through Integrative Thinking* (Boston: Harvard Business School Press, 2009).

27   Nathan Harter, "Leadership as the Promise of Simplification," *Emergence: Complexity and Organization* 8, no. 4 (2006).

28   Anuraj Gambhir is often attributed with popularizing the term *simplexity*. Jeffery Kluger wrote a book with that title, which I commend to the reader.

29   Alfred N. Whitehead, *The Concept of Nature* (Cambridge: University Press, 1920), 143.

30   Alfred Korzybski, "Science and Sanity: An Introduction to Non-Aristotelian Systems and General Semantics," paper presented at a meeting of the

American Association for the Advancement of Science (New Orleans: 1933).

31   George E. P. Box, "Science and Statistics," *Journal of the American Statistical Association* 71, 791–799.

32   Peter Senge, *The Fifth Discipline* (New York: Doubleday, 1990), 4.

33   Fritjof Capra, *The Systems View of Life: A Unifying Vision* (Cambridge: Cambridge University Press, 2014).

34   Arthur Koestler, *The Ghost in the Machine.* (New York: Penguin, 1967)

35   The use of superior and inferior is not meant in terms of importance or capability, but merely in terms of spatial reference within the holarchy.

36   W. Edwards Deming, *The New Economics for Industry, Government, and Education* (Boston: MIT Press, 1993), 50.

37   Max De Pree, *Leadership Is an Art* (New York: Dell, 1989), 145.

38   W. Edwards Deming, *The New Economics for Industry, Government, and Education* (Boston: MIT Press, 1993), 33.

39   W. Edwards Deming, *The New Economics for Industry, Government, and Education* (Boston: MIT Press, 1993).

40   Alfie Kohn, *Punished by Rewards: The Trouble with Gold Stars, Incentive Plans, A's, Praise, and Other Bribes* (New York, Houghton Mifflin, 1993).

41   Daniel H. Pink, *Drive: The Surprising Truth about What Motivates Us* (New York: Riverhead Books, 2011).

42   Eliyahu M. Goldratt, *The Goal: A Process of Ongoing Improvement* (Great Barrington: The North River Press, 1984).

43   For more information on the PDCA cycle see works by Deming and Walter Shewart.

44   Peter Senge, *The Fifth Discipline* (New York: Doubleday, 1990).

45   Margaret J. Wheatley, *Leadership and the New Science: Discovering Order in a Chaotic World* (San Francisco: Berrett-Koehler Publishers, 2006), 15.

46   Plato, *The Republic.*

47   Peter F. Drucker, "The Theory of the Business," *Harvard Business Review* (September–October 1994).

48   Mary Douglas, *How Institutions Think* (Syracuse, NY: Syracuse University Press, 1986), 92.

49   Mary Douglas, *How Institutions Think* (Syracuse, NY: Syracuse University Press, 1986), 92.

50   Todd D. Jick, *Managing Change: Cases and Concepts* (Boston, Irwin, 1993).

51   Alfred N. Whitehead, *Process and Reality: An Essay in Cosmology* (New York: McMillan, 1929).

52   Peter F. Drucker, "The Theory of the Business," *Harvard Business Review* (September–October Issue 1994).

53   John C. Maxwell, *The 5 Levels of Leadership*. Maxwell wrote, "Change is inevitable. Growth is optional."

54   The history of how the American Management Association (AMA) developed the six stars model was related to me by Paul Bradley, an AMA practitioner with whom I have worked for many years.

55   "Enduring Ideas: The 7-S Framework," *McKinsey Quarterly* (March 2008). Available at http://www.mckinsey.com/business-functions/strategy-and-corporate-finance/our-insights/enduring-ideas-the-7-s-framework.

56   Special thanks to my research assistants at Christopher Newport University: Travis Bruns, Lacey Martin, and Victoria Feola.

57   Applying rigorous selection criteria, the potential management frameworks were reduced to an initial set of 169 for further study. Using literature searches and review, these were further filtered leaving 71 management models for rigorous analysis. Next, the verbiage of every element of all 71 models was content analyzed for raw numbers of repetitions. These terms were further subjected to affinity analysis to eliminate overlap and concentrate on generalizable terms. In the next step of the research, the most common management models, as revealed by the literature searches and review, were specifically searched by name to determine frequency of citation.

58   All of these great management authors and others cautioned against treating the organization as a simple collection of elements.

59   Margaret J. Wheatley, *Leadership and the New Science: Discovering Order in a Chaotic World* (San Francisco: Berrett-Koehler Publishers, 2006), 164.

60   Xun Kuang (thought to have lived from 300–230 BC), also known as Xun Zi, was a philosopher in the Confucian tradition who contributed to parts of the Hundred Schools during the period known as the Warring States.

61   Jim Collins, *Good to Great: Why Some Companies Make the Leap and Others Don't* (New York: Harper Collins, 2001), 41.

62   Louis Pasteur, the inventor of the process of pasteurization was a French chemist and microbiologist.

63   Margaret J. Wheatley, *Leadership and the New Science: Discovering Order in a Chaotic World* (San Francisco: Berrett-Koehler Publishers, 2006), 138.

64   Gareth Morgan, *Images of Organizations* (Thousand Oaks: Sage Publications, 1997).

65   Max De Pree, *Leadership Is an Art* (New York: Dell, 1989), 55.

66   James Harvey Robinson, *The Mind in the Making: The Relation of Intelligence to Social Reform* (London: Cape, 1921).

67   W. V. Quine and J. S. Ullian, *The Web of Belief,* 2nd ed. (Columbus: McGraw-Hill College, 1978), 6.

68   Mary Douglas, *How Institutions Think* (Syracuse, NY: Syracuse University Press, 1986), 4.

69   *Henry the Fourth,* Part 2 Act 3, scene 1, 26–31.

70   Max De Pree, *Leadership Is an Art,* (New York: Dell, 1989), 3.

71   Daniel Goleman, *Emotional Intelligence: Why It Can Matter More Than IQ* (New York: Bantam, 1995).

72   Dr. Mehrabian found in some circumstances upwards of 93 percent of the information in a communication is imparted through tone of voice and body language. This phenomenon is easily understood by watching two dogs preparing to fight. There are no words, and often no tone, but what is about to happen is clear.

73   Charles S. Peirce, "The Fixation of Belief," *Popular Science Monthly* 12 (November, 1877): 1–15.

74   I heartily recommend IDEO's Design Thinking approach. You can find information at https://www.ideo.com/.

75   Edward de Bono, *Six Thinking Hats* (Boston: Little, Brown and Co., 1985).

76   Tara Swart, Kitty Chisholm, and Paul Brown in *Neuroscience for Leadership: Harnessing the Brain Gain Advantage* (New York: Palgrave Macmillan, 2015).

77   Max De Pree, *Leadership Is an Art* (New York: Dell, 1989).

78   Jim Collins, *Good to Great: Why Some Companies Make the Leap and Others Don't* (New York: Harper Collins, 2001), 20.

79   Jim Collins, *Good to Great: Why Some Companies Make the Leap and Others Don't* (New York: Harper Collins, 2001), 21.

80   Margaret J. Wheatley, *Leadership and the New Science: Discovering Order in a Chaotic World* (San Francisco: Berrett-Koehler Publishers, 2006), 164.

81   Jill Janov, *The Inventive Organization: Hope & Daring at Work* (San Francisco: Jossey-Bass, 1994).

82   Peter F. Drucker. *The Essential Drucker: The Best Sixty Years of Peter Drucker's Essential Writings on Management* (New York: Harper, 2001).

83   Terry Deal and Alan Kennedy, *Corporate Cultures: The Rites and Rituals of Corporate Life* (New York: Penguin, 1982).

84   http://www.gallup.com/poll/181289/majority-employees-not-engaged-despite-gains-2014.aspx.

85   Information about training expenditures can be found at http://www.
     trainingindustry.com/, and many other sources.

86   Charlie was a friend and fellow consultant who repeated that line often in
     our public session. He has a star on the American Management Association
     Wall of Fame next to Peter Drucker.

87   Tara Swart, Kitty Chisholm, and Paul Brown, *Neuroscience for Leadership*
     (Palgrave MacMillan, 2015).

88   Noel Burch, "Four Stages for Learning Any New Skill," a theory was
     developed at Gordon Training International (1970).

89   Peter Senge, *The Fifth Discipline* (New York: Doubleday, 1990).

90   This story was told to me during a management training session in Palm
     Springs, California, in 1993.

91   Robert Tannenbaum and Warren H. Schmidt, "How to Choose a
     Leadership Pattern," *Harvard Business Review* (May, 1973).

92   Source: Lee Ginzburg, Miller Ginzburg.

93   Miles Menander Dawson, *The Basic Teachings of Confucius* (New York:
     Garden City Publishing, 1942), 103.

94   Max De Pree, *Leadership Is an Art* (New York: Dell, 1989),145.

95   Margaret J. Wheatley, *Leadership and the New Science: Discovering Order in a
     Chaotic World* (San Francisco: Berrett-Koehler Publishers, 2006), 87.

96   Peter Senge, *The Fifth Discipline* (New York: Doubleday, 1990), 8–9.

97   Christopher A. Bartlett and Sumantra Ghoshal, "Beyond Strategy to
     Purpose," *Harvard Business Review* (November–December, 1994).

98   Jack Stack and Bo Burlingham, *The Great Game of Business: The Only
     Sensible Way to Run a Company* (New York: Doubleday, 1992). Stack
     championed the idea of "Open Book Management," sharing all important
     data broadly with employees.

99   Chris Argyris, "Double Loop Learning in Organizations," *Harvard Business
     Review* (September 1977).

100 Drucker does not show his theory graphically, so many managers miss the
     critical role assumptions play in driving subsequent mission, strategy, and
     action. Yet assumptions are the entire basis for the next step of formulating a
     mission or purpose.

101 Mary Douglas, *How Institutions Think* (Syracuse, NY: Syracuse University
     Press, 1986), 111.

102 Alfred N. Whitehead, *The Principles of Natural Knowledge* (Cambridge:
     University Press, 1919), 143.

103 Google's OKR process is described in a video on You Tube, https://www. youtube.com/watch?v=mJB83EZtAjc.

104 Margaret J. Wheatley, *Leadership and the New Science: Discovering Order in a Chaotic World* (San Francisco: Berrett-Koehler Publishers, 2006), 181.

105 Charles Handy, *The Age of Unreason* (London: Arrow, 2002).

106 Alfred D. Chandler Jr., *Strategy and Structure: Chapters in the History of the American Industrial Enterprise* (Cambridge: MIT Press, 1962).

107 Mary Douglas, *How Institutions Think* (Syracuse, NY: Syracuse University Press, 1986), 102.

108 Margaret J. Wheatley, *Leadership and the New Science: Discovering Order in a Chaotic World* (San Francisco: Berrett-Koehler Publishers, 2006).

109 Tara Swart, Kitty Chisholm, and Paul Brown, *Neuroscience for Leadership* (Palgrave MacMillan, 2015).

110 George D. Stoddard, a former commissioner of education in New York State. Dr. Stoddard was an educator who wrote extensively about the way we learn. He served as chancellor of New York University, and of Long Island University, president of the University of Illinois and president of the University of the State of New York, predecessor of the State University.

111 Jim Collins, *Good to Great: Why Some Companies Make the Leap and Others Don't* (New York: Harper Collins, 2001), 13.

112 Peter F. Drucker, *The Essential Drucker: The Best Sixty Years of Peter Drucker's Essential Writings on Management* (New York: Harper, 2001).

113 Margaret J. Wheatley, *Leadership and the New Science: Discovering Order in a Chaotic World* (San Francisco: Berrett-Koehler Publishers, 2006), 102.

114 Elisabeth Kübler-Ross, *On Grief and Grieving: Finding the Meaning of Grief Through the Five Stages of Loss* (New York: Scribner, 2005).

115 Leon Festinger, "Cognitive Dissonance," *Scientific American* 207, no. 4 (1962): 93–107.

116 Charles S. Peirce, "The Fixation of Belief," *Popular Science Monthly* 12 (November, 1877): 1–15.

117 Russell Eisenstat, Bert Spector, and Michael Beer, "Why Change Programs Don't Produce Change," *Harvard Business Review* (November–December 1990).

118 Michael Hammer and James Champy, *Reengineering the Corporation: A Manifesto for Business Revolution* (New York: Harper Collins, 2001).

119 https://www.apqc.org/.

120 William M. Donaldson, "An Examination of the Role of Enterprise Architecture Frameworks in Enterprise Transformation," *The Journal of Enterprise Transformation* 5, no. 3 (2015).

121 For more information on the du Pont identity, sometimes called the du Pont equation, see http://www.investopedia.com/terms/d/dupontidentity.asp.

122 The Family Firm Institute is an invaluable resource for family firms and family members. http://www.ffi.org.

123 Williams and Preisser, The Williams Group. Quoted in Forbes Personal Finance, http://www.forbes.com/sites/carolynrosenblatt/2011/12/09/wealth-transfers-how-to-reverse-the-70-failure-rate/#15318ca96044, 2013.

124 Peter Senge, *The Fifth Discipline* (New York: Doubleday, 1990), 12.

125 Peter Senge, *The Fifth Discipline* (New York: Doubleday, 1990), 266.

126 Miles Menander Dawson, *The Basic Teachings of Confucius* (New York: Garden City Publishing, 1942).

Morgan James
Speakers Group

www.TheMorganJamesSpeakersGroup.com

We connect Morgan James published
authors with live and online events
and audiences whom will benefit
from their expertise.

Morgan James makes all of our titles available
through the Library for All Charity Organizations.

www.LibraryForAll.org

Printed in the USA
CPSIA information can be obtained
at www.ICGtesting.com
JSHW022333140824
68134JS00019B/1463